English as a Global Language

English as a Global Language

Mrinal K Ghosh

AUTHORSPRESS

Worldwide Circulation through Authorspress Global Network
First Published 2009
by
Authorspress
E-35/103, Jawahar Park
Laxmi Nagar, Delhi-110 092
e-mail: authorspress@yahoo.com

English as a Global Language
ISBN 978-81-7273-492-3

Printed in India at Tarun Offset, Delhi.

Preface

English is a truly global language crossing many international boundaries. The language is so popular; it is spoken in more than a hundred countries and has more than a million words. English began its development in Great Britain and was spread across the globe through the colonial nations. It became so influential across the world that many countries adopted English above and beyond their own languages. The speed and depth with which the English language became so popular globally is unbelievable.

English has an inherent simplicity and flexibility allowing it to be learnt quickly, cementing English as a global language. The language is pretty simple to use, with clear grammatical rules governing nouns, verbs, adjectives etc. Because of these simple under-pinning rules, it is also an easy language to teach. The main feature of the English language that has made is so popular globally, is the language's adaptability. The language has taken on words from many other languages and cultures, giving it its great diversity. There are many German, Greek, Latin and French words that have been assimilated by the English language.

English is an official language of the United Nations and many other international organisations, including the International Olympic Committee. About 85 per cent of all written material in the world is written in English. No matter where you are in the world, English is a global language and once you should really consider mastering. By learning English, one can get a better job, have a better career but more importantly, keep up-to-date with world events and developments.

This book presents a lively and informative account of the rise of English as a global language. It includes a historical summary of the global development of English, the current spread and status of English as a first and second language internationally, and the future potential of English as the international language of communication. The contents of the book will be highly valuable to all the lovers and learners of English.

Mrinal K Ghosh

Contents

1

Historical Development of English Language

1.1. Origin of English

English is a member of the Indo-European family of languages. This broad family includes most of the European languages spoken today. The Indo-European family includes several major branches:

- Latin and the modern Romance languages;
- The Germanic languages;
- The Indo-Iranian languages, including Hindi and Sanskrit;
- The Slavic languages;
- The Baltic languages of Latvian and Lithuanian (but not Estonian);
- The Celtic languages; and
- Greek.

The influence of the original Indo-European language, designated proto-Indo-European, can be seen today, even though no written record of it exists. The word for father, for example, is vater in German, pater in Latin, and pitr in Sanskrit. These words are all cognates, similar words in different languages that share the same root.

Of these branches of the Indo-European family, two are, for our purposes of studying the development of English, of paramount importance, the Germanic and the Romance (called that because the Romance languages derive from Latin, the language of ancient Rome, not because of any bodice-ripping literary genre). English is in the Germanic group of languages. This group began as a common language in the Elbe river region about 3,000 years ago. Around the second century BC, this Common Germanic language split into three distinct sub-groups:

- East Germanic was spoken by peoples who migrated back to southeastern Europe. No East Germanic language is spoken today, and the only written East Germanic language that survives is Gothic.
- North Germanic evolved into the modern Scandinavian languages of Swedish, Danish, Norwegian, and Icelandic (but not Finnish, which is related to Estonian and is not an Indo-European language).
- West Germanic is the ancestor of modern German, Dutch, Flemish, Frisian, and English.

English is a West Germanic language which originated from the Anglo-Frisian dialects brought to Britain by Germanic settlers and Roman auxiliary troops from various parts of what is now northwest Germany and the northern Netherlands. Initially, Old English was a diverse group of dialects, reflecting the varied origins of the Anglo-Saxon Kingdoms of England. One of these dialects, Late West Saxon, eventually came to dominate. The original Old English language was then influenced by two waves of invasion: the first by speakers of the Scandinavian branch of the Germanic language family, who conquered and colonised parts of Britain in the 8th and 9th centuries; the second by the Normans in the 11th century, who spoke Old Norman and ultimately developed an English variety of this called Anglo-Norman. These two invasions caused English to become "mixed" to some degree, though it was never a truly mixed language in the strict linguistic sense of the word, as mixed languages arise from the cohabitation of speakers of different languages, who develop a hybrid tongue for basic communication.

Cohabitation with the Scandinavians resulted in a significant grammatical simplification and lexical enrichment of the Anglo-Frisian core of English; the later Norman occupation led to the grafting onto that Germanic core of a more elaborate layer of words from the Romance languages. This Norman influence entered English largely through the courts and government. Thus, English developed into a "borrowing" language of great flexibility, resulting in an enormous and varied vocabulary.

1.1.1. Proto-English

The Germanic tribes that gave rise to the English language (the Angles, Saxons, Frisians, Jutes and perhaps even the Franks), both traded and fought with the Latin-speaking Roman Empire in the centuries-long process of the Germanic peoples' expansion into Western Europe. Many Latin words for common objects entered the vocabulary of these Germanic peoples before any of their tribes reached Britain; examples include camp, cheese, cook, fork, inch, kettle, kitchen, linen, mile, mill, mint (coin), noon, pillow, pin, pound, punt (boat), street and wall. The Romans also gave the English language words which they had themselves borrowed from other languages: anchor, butter, chest, devil, dish, sack and wine.

Our main source for the culture of the Germanic peoples (the ancestors of the English) in ancient times is Tacitus' Germania. While remaining quite conversant with Roman civilisation and its economy, including serving in the Roman military, they retained political independence. We can be certain that Germanic settlement in Britain was not intensified until the time of Hengist and Horsa in the fifth century, since had the English arrived en-masse under Roman rule, they would have been thoroughly Christianised as a matter of course. As it was, the Angles, Saxons and Jutes arrived as pagans, independent of Roman control.

1.1.2. Old English

Old English is an early form of the English language that was spoken and written in parts of what are now England and southern Scotland between the mid-5th century and the mid-12th century. What survives through writing represents primarily the literary register of Anglo-Saxon. It is a West Germanic language and is closely related to Old Frisian. It also experienced heavy influence from Old Norse, a member of the related North Germanic group of languages.

Old English was not static, and its usage covered a period of approximately 700 years—from the Anglo-Saxon migrations that created England in the fifth century to some time after the Norman invasion of 1066, when the language underwent a dramatic transition. During this early period it assimilated some aspects of the languages with which it came in contact, such as the Celtic languages and the two dialects of Old Norse from the invading Vikings, who were occupying and controlling large tracts of land in northern and eastern England, which came to be known as the Danelaw.

1.1.2.1. Germanic origins

The most important force in shaping Old English was its Germanic heritage in its vocabulary, sentence structure and grammar, which it shared with its sister languages in continental Europe. Some of these features were specific to the West Germanic language family to which Old English belongs, while some other features were inherited from the Proto-Germanic language from which all Germanic languages are believed to have derived.

Like other West Germanic languages of the period, Old English was fully inflected with five grammatical cases (nominative, accusative, genitive, dative, and instrumental, though the instrumental was very rare), which had dual plural forms for referring to groups of two objects (but only in the personal pronouns) in addition to the usual singular and plural forms. It also assigned gender to all nouns, including those that describe inanimate objects: for example, seo sunne (the Sun) was feminine, while se mona (the Moon) was masculine.

1.1.2.2. Latin influence

A large percentage of the educated and literate population of their time (monks, clerics, etc.) were competent in Latin, which was the scholarly and diplomatic lingua franca of Europe at the time. It is sometimes possible to give approximate dates for the entry of individual Latin words into Old English based on which patterns of linguistic change they have undergone. There were at least three notable periods of Latin influence. The first occurred before the ancestral Saxons left continental Europe for Britain. The second began when the Anglo-Saxons were converted to Christianity and Latin-speaking priests became widespread. The third and largest single transfer of Latin-based words happened after the Norman invasion of 1066, after which an enormous number of Norman words entered the language. Most of these Oïl language words were themselves derived from Old French and ultimately from classical Latin, although a notable stock of Norse words were introduced or re-introduced in Norman form. The Norman Conquest approximately marks the end of Old English and the advent of Middle English.

One of the ways the influence of Latin can be seen is that many Latin words for activities came to also be used to refer to the people engaged in those activities, an idiom carried over from Anglo-Saxon but using Latin words. This can be seen in words like militia, assembly, movement, and service. The language was further altered by the transition away from the runic alphabet (also known as futhorc or fuþorc) to the Latin alphabet, which was also a significant factor in the developmental pressures brought to bear on the language. Old English words were spelt as they were pronounced; the "silent" letters in many Modern English words, such as the k in knight, were in fact pronounced in Old English. For example, the c in cniht, the Old English ancestor of the modern knight, was pronounced. Another side-effect of spelling words phonetically was that spelling was extremely variable—the spelling of a word would reflect differences in the phonetics of the writer's regional dialect, and also idiosyncratic spelling choices which varied from author to author, and even from work to work by the same author. Thus, for example, the word and could be spelt either and or ond.

1.1.2.3. Norse influence

The second major source of loanwords to Old English was the Scandinavian words introduced during the Viking invasions of the 9th and 10th centuries. In addition to a great many place names, these consist mainly of items of basic vocabulary, and words concerned with particular administrative aspects of the Danelaw (that is, the area of land under Viking control, which included extensive holdings all along the eastern coast of England and Scotland). The Vikings spoke Old Norse, a language related to Old English in that both derived from the same ancestral Proto-Germanic language. It is very common for the intermixing of speakers of different dialects, such as those that occur during times of political unrest, to result in a mixed language, and one theory holds that exactly such a mixture of Old Norse and Old English helped accelerate the decline of case endings in Old English. Apparent confirmation of this is the fact that simplification of the case endings occurred earliest in the North and latest in the Southwest, the area farthest away from Viking influence. Regardless of the truth of this theory, the influence of Old Norse on the English language has been profound: responsible for such basic vocabulary items as sky, leg, the pronoun they, the verb form are, and hundreds of other words.

1.1.2.4. Celtic influence

Traditionally, many maintain that the influence of Celtic on English has been small, citing the small number of Celtic loanwords taken into the language. The number of Celtic loanwords is of a lower order than either Latin or Scandinavian; distinctive Celtic traits have been argued to be clearly discernible from the post-Old English period in the area of syntax.

1.1.2.5. Dialects

Old English should not be regarded as a single monolithic entity just as Modern English is also not monolithic. Within Old English, there was language variation. Thus, it is misleading, for example, to consider Old English as having a single sound system. Rather, there were multiple Old English sound systems. Old English has variation along regional lines as well as variation across different times. For example, the language attested in West Saxon during the time of thelwold of Winchester, which is named Late West Saxon (or thelwoldian Saxon), is considerably different from the language attested in West Saxon during the time of Alfred the Great's court, which is named Early West Saxon (or Classical West Saxon or Alfredian Saxon). Furthermore, the difference between Early West Saxon and Late West Saxon is of such a nature that Late West Saxon is not directly descended from Early West Saxon (despite what the similarity in name implies).

The four main dialectal forms of Old English were Mercian, Northumbrian (known collectively as Anglian), Kentish, and West Saxon. Each of those dialects was associated with an independent kingdom on the island. Of these, all of Northumbria and most of Mercia were overrun by the Vikings during the 9th century. The portion of Mercia and all of Kent that were successfully defended were then integrated into Wessex.

After the process of unification of the diverse Anglo-Saxon kingdoms in 878 by Alfred the Great, there is a marked decline in the importance of regional dialects. This is not because they stopped existing; regional dialects continued even after that time to this day, as evidenced both by the existence of middle and modern English dialects later on, and by common sense - people do not spontaneously adopt another dialect when there is a sudden change of political power.

However, the bulk of the surviving documents from the Anglo-Saxon period are written in the dialect of Wessex, Alfred's kingdom. It seems likely that with consolidation of power, it became necessary to standardise the language of government to reduce the difficulty of administering the more remote areas of the kingdom. As a result, paperwork was written in the West Saxon dialect. Not only this, but Alfred was passionate about the spread of the vernacular and brought many scribes to his region from Mercia in order that previously unwritten texts be recorded.

The Church was affected likewise, especially since Alfred initiated an ambitious programme to translate religious materials into English. In order to retain his patronage and ensure the widest circulation of the translated materials, the monks and priests engaged in the programme worked in his dialect. Alfred himself seems to have translated books out of Latin and into English, notably Pope Gregory I's treatise on administration, "Pastoral Care". Because of the centralisation of power and the Viking invasions, there is little or no written evidence for the development of non-Wessex dialects after Alfred's unification.

1.1.3. Middle English

For about 300 years following the Norman Conquest in 1066, the Norman kings and their high nobility spoke only one of the langues d'oïl called Anglo-Norman, whilst English continued to be the language of the common people. Various contemporary sources suggest that within fifty years of the invasion, most of the Normans outside the royal court spoke English, with French remaining the prestige language of government and law, largely out of social inertia. For example, Orderic Vitalis, a historian born in 1075 and the son of a Norman knight, said that he learned French only as a second language. A tendency for French-derived words to have more formal connotations has continued to the present day; most modern English speakers would consider a "cordial reception" (from French) to be more formal than a "hearty welcome" (Germanic). Another example is the very unusual construction of the words for animals being separate from the words for their food products e.g. beef and pork (from the French boeuf and porc) being the products of the Germanically-named animals 'cow' and 'pig'.

While the Anglo-Saxon Chronicle continued until 1154, most other literature from this period was in Old Norman or Latin. A large number of Norman words were taken into Old English, with many doubling for Old English words. The Norman influence is the hallmark of the linguistic shifts in English over the period of time following the invasion, producing what is now referred to as Middle English. English was also influenced by the Celtic languages it was displacing, most notably with the introduction of the continuous aspect, a feature found in many modern languages, but developed earlier and more thoroughly in English. English spelling was also influenced by Norman in this period, with the /θ/ and /ð/ sounds being spelled th rather than with the Old English letters þ (thorn) and ð (eth), which did not exist in Norman.

1.1.4. Early Modern English

Modern English is often dated from the Great Vowel Shift, which took place mainly during the 15th century. English was further transformed by the spread of a standardised London-based dialect in government and administration and by the standardising effect of printing. By the time of William Shakespeare (mid-late 16th century), the language had become clearly recognisable as Modern English.

English has continuously adopted foreign words, especially from Latin and Greek, since the Renaissance. As there are many words from different languages and English spelling is variable, the risk of mispronunciation is high, but remnants of the older forms remain in a few regional dialects, most notably in the West Country. In 1755, Samuel Johnson published the first significant English dictionary, his *Dictionary of the English Language.*

1.1.5. Late Modern English (1800-Present)

The main difference between Early Modern English and Late Modern English is vocabulary. Late Modern English has many more words, arising from two principal factors: firstly, the Industrial Revolution and technology created a need for new words; secondly, the British Empire at its height covered one quarter of the earth's surface, and the English language adopted foreign words from many countries.

1.2. Vocabulary of English Language

The vocabulary of English language is a mixture of Germanic (Old English and Scandinavian), Greek, Latin and French where almost half of it is Germanic and Greek and half is Latin and French with some of the words from almost all of the notable languages of the world as it had taken free admission from everywhere.

In 1864 Frederick James Furnivall founded the Early English Text Society to initiate the revival of the Medieval English literature and to synchronise it with the gradual development of the English language. As a result of that "A New English Dictionary on Historical Principles," edited by Sir James A.H. Murray and assisted by three more editors, Bradley, Charles Onions and Craigie, was published in 12 volumes along with its supplements from 1884 to 1928. It gives the inventory and the history of words in use from 1150 up to 1500 of all the five dialects of the Middle English. After 1500 only literary English words are taken, not the dialecticals. It enormously contains the quotations from the English literature and records, and incorporates the words that have entered into English vocabulary from the earliest records to the existing date along with their history and origin. It contains more than 15,000 pages and over 400,000 words. A revised and concise edition of this dictionary called "*The Oxford English Dictionary*" was first published in 1933.

1.3. Varieties of English

From around 1600, the English colonisation of North America resulted in the creation of a distinct American variety of English. Some English pronunciations and words "froze" when they reached America. In some ways, American English is more like the English of Shakespeare than modern British English is. Some expressions that the British call "Americanisms" are in fact original British expressions that were preserved in the colonies while lost for a time in Britain (for example trash for rubbish, loan as a verb instead of lend, and fall for autumn; another example, frame-up, was re-imported into Britain through Hollywood gangster movies). Spanish also had an influence on American English (and subsequently British English), with words like canyon, ranch, stampede and vigilante being examples of Spanish words that entered English through the settlement of the American West. French words (through Louisiana) and West African words (through the slave trade) also influenced American English (and so, to an extent, British English).

Today, American English is particularly influential, due to the USA's dominance of cinema, television, popular music, trade and technology (including the Internet). But there are many other varieties of English around the world, including for example Australian English, New Zealand English, Canadian English, South African English, Indian English and Caribbean English.

1.4. Shaping English Language

Philip Durkin, Principal etymologist at the Oxford English Dictionary, chooses five events that shaped the English Language.

1.4.1. Anglo-Saxon Settlement

It's never easy to pinpoint exactly when a specific language began, but in the case of English we can at least say that there is little sense in speaking of the English language as a separate entity before the Anglo-Saxons came to Britain. Little is known of this period with any certainty, but we do know that Germanic invaders came and settled in Britain from the north-western coastline of continental Europe in the fifth and sixth centuries. The invaders all spoke a language that was Germanic (related to what emerged as Dutch, Frisian, German and the Scandinavian languages, and to Gothic), but we'll probably never know how different their speech was from that of their continental neighbours. However it is fairly certain that many of the settlers would have spoken in exactly the same way as some of their north European neighbours, and that not all of the settlers would have spoken in the same way.

The reason that we know so little about the linguistic situation in this period is because we do not have much in the way of written records from any of the Germanic languages of north-western Europe until several centuries later. When Old English writings begin to appear in the seventh, eighth and ninth centuries there is a good deal of regional variation, but not substantially more than that found in later periods. This was the language that Alfred the Great referred to as 'English' in the ninth century.

The Celts were already resident in Britain when the Anglo-Saxons arrived, but there are few obvious traccs of their language in English today. Some scholars have suggested that the Celtic tongue might have had an underlying influence on the grammatical development of English, particularly in some parts of the country, but this is highly speculative. The number of loanwords known for certain to have entered Old English from this source is very small. Those that survive in modern English include brock (badger), and coomb a type of valley, alongside many place names.

1.4.2. Scandinavian Settlements

The next invaders were the Norsemen. From the middle of the ninth century large numbers of Norse invaders settled in Britain, particularly in northern and eastern areas, and in the eleventh century the whole of England had a Danish king, Canute. The distinct North Germanic speech of the Norsemen had great influence on English, most obviously seen in the words that English has borrowed from this source. These include some very basic words such as take and even grammatical words such as they. The common Germanic base of the two languages meant that there were still many similarities between Old English and the language of the invaders. Some words, for example give perhaps show a kind of hybridisation with some spellings going back to Old English and others being Norse in origin. However, the resemblances between the two languages are so great that in many cases it is impossible to be sure of the exact ancestry of a particular word or spelling. However, much of the influence of Norse, including the vast majority of the loanwords, does not appear in written English until after the next great historical and cultural upheaval, the Norman Conquest.

1.4.3. 1066 and after 1066 and all that

The centuries after the Norman Conquest witnessed enormous changes in the English language. In the course of what is called the Middle English period, the fairly rich inflectional system of Old English broke down. It was replaced by what is broadly speaking, the same system English has today, which unlike Old English makes very little use of distinctive word endings in the grammar of the language. The vocabulary of English also changed enormously, with tremendous numbers of borrowings from French and Latin, in addition to the Scandinavian loanwords already mentioned, which were slowly starting to appear in the written language. Old English, like German today, showed a tendency to find native equivalents for foreign words and phrases (although both Old English and modern German show plenty of loanwords), whereas Middle English acquired the habit that modern English retains today of readily accommodating foreign words. Trilingualism in English, French, and Latin was common in the worlds of business and the professions, with words crossing over from one language to another with ease. One only has to flick through the etymologies of any English dictionary to get an impression of the huge number of words entering English from French and Latin during the later medieval period. This trend was set to continue into the early modern period with the explosion of interest in the writings of the ancient world.

1.4.4. Standardisation

The late medieval and early modern periods saw a fairly steady process of standardisation in English south of the Scottish border. The written and spoken language of London continued to evolve and gradually began to have a greater influence in the country at large. For most of the Middle English period a dialect was simply what was spoken in a particular area, which would normally be more or less represented in writing—although where and from whom the writer had learnt how to write were also important. It was only when the broadly London standard began to dominate, especially through the new technology of printing, that the other regional varieties of the language began to be seen as different in kind. As the London standard became used more widely, especially in more formal contexts and particularly amongst the more elevated members of society, the other regional varieties came to be stigmatised, as lacking social prestige and indicating a lack of education.

In the same period a series of changes also occurred in English pronunciation (though not uniformly in all dialects), which go under the collective name of the Great Vowel Shift. These were purely linguistic 'sound changes' which occur in every language in every period of history. The changes in pronunciation weren't the result of specific social or historical factors, but social and historical factors would have helped to spread the results of the changes. As a result the so-called 'pure' vowel sounds which still characterise many continental languages were lost to English. The phonetic pairings of most long and short vowel sounds were also lost, which gave rise to many of the oddities of English pronunciation, and which now obscure the relationships between many English words and their foreign counterparts.

1.4.5. Colonisation and Globalisation

During the medieval and early modern periods the influence of English spread throughout the British Isles, and from the early seventeenth century onwards its influence began to be felt throughout the world. The complex processes of exploration, colonisation and overseas trade that characterised Britain's external relations for several centuries became agents for change in the English language. This wasn't simply through the acquisition of loanwords deriving from languages from every corner of the world, which in many cases only entered English via the languages of other trading and imperial nations such as Spain, Portugal and the Netherlands, but through the gradual development of new varieties of English, each with their own nuances of vocabulary and grammar and their own distinct pronunciations. More recently still, English has become a lingua franca, a global language, regularly used and understood by many nations for whom English is not their first language. The eventual effects on the English language of both of these developments can only be guessed at today, but there can be little doubt that they will be as important as anything that has happened to English in the past sixteen hundred years.

1.5. Evolutionary Development of English

The English language begins with the Anglo-Saxons. The Romans, who had controlled England for centuries, had withdrawn their troops and most of their colonists by the early 400s. Attacks from the Irish, the Picts from Scotland, the native Britons, and Anglo-Saxons from across the North Sea, plus the deteriorating situation in the rest of the Empire, made the retreat a strategic necessity. As the Romans withdrew, the Britons re-established themselves in the western parts of England, and the Anglo-Saxons invaded and began to settle the eastern parts in the middle 400s. The Britons are the ancestors of the modern day Welsh, as well as the people of Britanny across the English channel. The Anglo-Saxons apparently displaced or absorbed the original Romanised Britons, and created the five kingdoms of Northumbria, Mercia, Kent, East Anglia, Essex, Sussex, and Wessex. Notice that the last three are actually contractions of East Saxon, South Saxon, and West Saxon, and that the Welsh still refer to the English as Saxons (*Saesneg*).

The language we now call English is actually a blend of many languages. Even the original Anglo-Saxon was already a blend of the dialects of west Germanic tribes living along the North Sea coast: The Saxons in Germany and eastern Holland, the Jutes, possibly from northern Denmark (the area now called Jutland), and the Angles, probably living along the coast and on islands between Denmark and Holland. It is also likely that the invaders included Frisians from northern Holland and northern Franks from southern Holland (whose relatives gave their name to France). The dialects were close enough for each to understand the other.

Later, in the 800s, the Northmen (Vikings) came to England, mostly from Denmark, and settled in with the Anglo-Saxons from Yorkshire to Norfolk, an area that became known as the Danelaw. Others from Norway ruled over the people in the northwest, from Strathclyde to the north of Wales. The Norse language they spoke resembled Anglo-Saxon in many ways, but was different enough for two things to happen: One, there were many Old Norse words that entered into English, including even such basic ones as they and them; And two, the complex conjugations and declensions began to wither away as people disagreed about which to use!

Last, William the Conqueror and his Norman supporters invaded England in 1066. Although, as their name suggests, they were the descendents of the same Northmen that had invaded England earlier, they had been settled long enough in Normandy in the north of France to adopt a dialect of French. They brought this Norman French with them to England and kept it as the language of their newly imposed aristocracy. In the day-to-day need to communicate, the common language became English, but with a large number of French words, and still more withering of grammatical complexities.

English since then has been absorbing vocabulary from a huge number of sources. French, the language of diplomacy for Europe for centuries, Latin, the language of the church, and Greek, the language of philosophy and science, contributed many words, especially the more "educated" ones. Other European languages have left culturally specific words. The American Indian languages, Australian Aborigine languages, and the languages of Africa and India gave us many hundreds of words, especially for the innumerable species of plants and animals of the world. On top of all this, there is the steady creation of new words and new uses for old words by the many subcultures of the English speaking world.

1.6. Advanced English Language

The English language is considered to be the world language of today. It has an extensive amount of words not found in other languages and its rich vocabulary may sufficiently accommodate all the situations of a social and technical nature. But, even at the maximum height of its evolution could you be sure of the spellings of the names of people or their pronunciations unless you are told? Isn't it a dilemma that the vowels have no fixed sound or phonetic value, like, father, eye, now, son, sun, where a, e, o and u, all of them sound as a, (long or short), and o is either o or a as in Joan, John, Johnny? It is because the basic alphabetic structure was scientifically wrong from the very beginning; and this is the case with all other languages of the world.

References

Baugh, Albert C, Thomas Cable, *A history of the English language*, 5th ed., Routledge, 2002.

Bragg, Melvyn, *The Adventure of English: The Biography of a Language*, Arcade Publishing, 2004.

Crystal, David, *English as a Global Language*, Cambridge: Cambridge University Press, 1997.

________________, *The Cambridge encyclopedia of the English language*, 2nd ed., Cambridge University Press, 2003.

McArthur, T. (ed.), *The Oxford Companion to the English Language*, Oxford University Press, 1992.

Robinson, Orrin, *Old English and Its Closest Relatives*, Stanford Univ. Press, 1992.

2

Spread of English

In 1914 M. Follick envisioned the global spread of a simplified form of English. Today, his vision has been enormously surpassed: English is used as the global language—spoken in all fields which require international contact and co-operation. It therefore makes sense to give a short historical sketch of how this "spreading" of the language happened. The foundations for the expansion of English were laid as the British Empire itself expanded. English and English Language Teaching (ELT) served as a tool to strengthen British rule. The result of colonial education policies was the creation of an English speaking native elite on the one side and a vernacular speaking majority on the other.

2.1. Different Approaches and Terminology

Different linguists have provided a variety of labels to categorise the spread of English. Although these labels all describe the same phenomenon they are by no means synonyms; rather, they exemplify different theoretical backgrounds and different approaches. Traditionally, a distinction has been made between ESL (English as a Second Language) countries, where the language has official status, EFL (English as a Foreign Language) countries where this is not the case, and ENL (English as a native language) countries. However, this model has recently been criticised because it is difficult to apply in a context of multilingualism.

Another classic model is Kachru's distinction of three concentric circles of English with an Inner Circle (containing the US, the UK, Canada, Australia and New Zealand), an Outer Circle and an Expanding Circle. More recently, Kachru has introduced the term "English using speech-fellowships". He distinguishes between three types of such fellowships, namely norm providing, norm-developing (the Outer Circle) and norm-dependent fellowships. He also notes that until recently the British model was the preferred one for the norm-dependent fellowship but this is slowly changing in favour of American English.

Another term coined by Kachru is "World Englishes". Although the linguistic right sees the term itself as a proof of slipping standards, mainstream linguistics has accepted this terminology. According to Kachru the concept "symbolises the functional and formal variations, divergent sociolinguistic contexts, ranges and varieties of English in creativity, and various types of acculturation...This concept emphasizes "WE-ness" and not the dichotomy between us and them."

Additionally, the abbreviation EIL (English as an international language) is often used. Modiano emphasises that in the teaching of EIL emphasis should be on a descriptive rather than a prescriptive model; this puts EIL in sharp contrast to the British English near-native speaker proficiency model promoted and practised in many parts of the world.

2.2. English as a Tool for Linguistic Imperialism

Robert Phillipson sees the promotion of English as a form of Western domination over developing countries. For him "the dominance of English is asserted and maintained by the establishment and continuos reconstitution of structural and cultural inequalities between English and other languages". Phillipson develops the concept of linguistic imperialism which occurs if the lives of the speakers of a language are dominated by another language to the point where they believe that they can and should use only that foreign language when it comes to transactions dealing with the more advanced aspects of life.

According to Phillipson, linguistic imperialism "takes place within an overarching structure of asymmetrical North/South relations, where language interlocks with other dimensions, cultural..., economic and political".

2.2.1. Tenets and Fallacies of ELT

Phillipson argues that the basic tenets upon which ELT is based favour linguistic imperialism. The first of these tenets—which, according to Phillipson, were worked out at the 1961 Makere conference—states that English is best taught monolingually. Other scholars agree with Phillipson that it is questionable to apply a monolingual approach to the multilingual situation in Africa or Asia. Generally, the problem is when an absolute virtue is made of local necessity by claims of global validity, when it is assumed that if the approach works here it ought to work, or made to work, everywhere else".

The second tenet holds that the ideal teacher is a native speaker. The notion of the native speaker is connected with the idea that only naturally occurring, or "authentic", language should be taught. Because authenticity can only be determined by insiders, only native speakers can teach it. The non-native speaker gains the advantage because he knows what is appropriate in the context of language learning. The problem is, however, that despite those findings, native speakers are still sent around the world.

The other tenets—or rather fallacies—are that "the earlier English is taught, the better the results", "the more English is thought, the better the results" and "if other languages are used much, standards of English will drop". The latter argument has been used to legitimate a continued British presence in former colonies, according to Phillipson.

2.2.2. Promoting the Spread of English

According to Phillipson those who promote English—that is organisations (like the British Council, the IMF and the World Bank) or single individuals, (those who operate English language schools, for instance)—use three types of argument:

- English intrinsic arguments describe the language as God-given, rich, noble and interesting. These arguments usually assert what English is and other languages are not.
- English extrinsic arguments point out that English is well established. There are trained teachers and a multitude of teaching material. There are also abundant immaterial resources like knowledge of the language.
- English functional arguments emphasise the usefulness of English as a gateway to the world.

Other arguments for English are:

– Its economic-reproductive function: it enables people to operate technology.
– Its ideological function: it stands for modernity.
– It is a symbol for material advance and efficiency.

2.3. As a Tool for International Understanding

David Crystal does not see English as an instrument of imperialism but as a tool which "presents us with unprecedented possibilities for mutual understanding". While Phillipson states his political purposes quite openly, Crystal claims to have written a book without any political agenda, a statement which raises suspicions because, as Phillipson rightly points out, "even the wish to be apolitical involves political choices". Crystal does admit that native speakers might be in a position of power but his solution is to teach English from early childhood on, a suggestion which is likely to enrage those who, like Phillipson, want more emphasis on education in native languages. Crystal offers interesting information about the spread of English—geographically, historically as well as in such functional domains as tourism and pop music. However, his evaluation of English always remains positive even if he gives facts which might seem worrying: for Crystal there is apparently nothing wrong with the fact that 70% out of 160 linguistic journals are published entirely in English. Even the fact that farmers from Sri Lanka cannot read the instructions on the bags of imported fertiliser—because they are in English—is only given to emphasise the need for comprehensive English teaching.

Crystal apparently does not see that, as more and more international communication takes place in the language of wider communication, other languages are in danger of being reduced to languages of "narrower communication". Crystal's emphasis on global understanding it is important to point out that English can also act as a medium and subject of global misunderstanding. Indeed, such misunderstandings may even occur between speakers of two varieties of English: in a study reported by Platt a group of English speaking Malaysian and Singaporean students had severe problems with communicative strategies used in Australia. They were, for instance, puzzled about the routine question "how'd you like it" in a bank because Singaporean and Malaysian bank tellers do not give customers the opportunity to choose what denominations of currency they would like (fives, tens, fifties...).

2.4. Influence of Capitalism in the Spread of English

In the 20 century the spread of English has continued because of the rising influence of the United States, which became the leading capitalist power. Today, English Language Teaching certainly is, as Pennycook puts it, not only good for business but also good business itself: 600.000 people come to Great Britain each year to learn English and in the course of doing so spend around 700 million pounds. British English language products alone are worth over 500 million pounds a year. It has been estimated that the world-wide EFL market is even worth 6.25 billion pounds. In countries which have recently opened up to the capitalist system, most importantly the nations of Eastern Europe and Asian countries like China and Vietnam, the demand for ELT has exploded. In these countries English is often learnt because it is the international language of money.

The implications of this "capitalisation" of English Language Teaching are;

Firstly, because ELT is such a big business, it is subject to market forces and to commercial policies.

Secondly, EFL material for the international market has been criticised for being too anglo-centric: for Marc Deineire, his students from Western Europe, South Amercia, Africa and Asia have one thing in common: "they all use the same books, the same dictionaries, the same grammars, all written by people who often have no idea of the linguistic and cultural reality of these countries". Moreover, such textbooks may present norms which are in direct conflict with local social and cultural standards. Muslims, for example, may take offence at the way ELT textbooks portray the interaction between men and women. In a corresponding counter-movement some governments have decided to use only indigenous material in ELT. In time, such non-native ELT material may be exported to other non-native countries where it will again be modified to suit local demands.

Thirdly, because more and more books in the natural sciences are published in English, students of those sciences now have to reach a high level of competence in English to pursue their studies. At the Technical University of Vienna, for instance, students of computer science have to take a certain number of courses in English and are additionally required to read technical literature in that language.

2.5. English for Elites

More dangerous than widespread ELT is ELT which is reserved for elites. A negative attitude towards English appears when perfect command of the language is seen as the symbol of a "small Brahmanic caste" while the masses are kept out. However, we must be aware that discrimination regarding access to English is only a symptom of wider societal tensions.

In the education system of some developing countries English is used as a means of selecting the pupils most "suitable" for higher education. However, the argument above answers Roger's question whether it is ethical to go on teaching English to so many children in the Third World when only few of them will get a job where they can use it. The answer must be that "yes, it is ethical" firstly, because, as Abbott points out, not teaching English would make those children even less employable and secondly, because not teaching English would only strengthen the local elite. In some parts of Asia, the English-educated group is seen as pseudo-westernised and as having non-Asian values. In regard to South Africa, de Kadt reports that those black students who spoke much English were perceived as being arrogant. One reason for this may be that English is often regarded as an "alchemy" for social change and those who fear this change project their fear onto English. But, as Kachru reveals, even among the anti-English faction the more pragmatic ones ensure that their own relatives are able to learn English.

2.5.1. International English and Intranational English

The future development of English is likely to be characterised by a contrast between a standard (or even standards) for international interaction and local varieties of English. The latter category has often been disregarded: it has been overlooked that besides being an international lingua franca, English is also used intranationally to impart local cultural traditions and values. Such intranational functions are the use of English in public education, in public administration, in science and technology, in the mass media and the entertainment industry and for literature.

It has been argued that local varieties of English will evolve into separate languages just as Latin did. However, because the present situation is unique it is risky to use analogies with past events. On the one hand English is spread more widely than Latin ever was and this could mean that local Englishes will dissolve into separate languages even faster than Latin did. On the other hand, the event which played a pivotal role in the transformation of Latin into other languages was, of course, the fall of the Roman Empire, its culture and civilisation. Today, by contrast, the position of the USA (the dominant English speaking power) does not seem threatened. One should also take into account that the Romans did not have the technical means to stay in communication with their far-flung provinces effectively. Modern means of transport, the global media and the internet may be counter-forces against fragmentation. Another unifying factor may be the global youth and pop culture, in which English plays an important role. However, the actual influence of these global forces on local Englishes is still uncertain.

Anyway, while these local forms of English (or intranational Englishes) will have a strong connection with community and identity, the standard for international transactions (international English) will be associated with communication and information. In a sense, international English has its communities too, for example the world-wide community of doctors, of lawyers, or of managers. However, in contrast to local communities, such communities are "dislocalised", that is they are not tied to a geographical location.

2.5.2. Standards of Non-native Englishes

When dealing with World Englishes the question of internal and external status is one that has to be dealt with. Regarding internal status, to begin with, we are confronted with a variety of different findings. Regarding the situation in Malaysia, for instance, Gill reports that an educated British English speaker with an RP accent is found most suitable. Furthermore, Crismore Ngeow and Soo report that Malaysian speakers of English see Malaysian English as "mistakes" that have to be eradicated. For the situation in Sri Lanka, by contrast, Passe elaborates that those who speak English like a native speaker would be unpopular, because their accent would be seen either as an indication that they belong to a favoured class or that they are trying to imitate their betters. Thus, it is the local socio-political context which has a crucial influence on the internal status of the local form of English. In South Africa, for instance, English had been associated with colonialism but came to be seen as the language of freedom during the Apartheid regime. In this respect, it is crucial how the scholar him or herself evaluates the socio-political context: a pro-apartheid scholar will probably report and evaluate findings from South-Africa very differently than a former resistance fighter.

With all these Englishes around, the question which standard should be used as a model is bound to arise. Surely, there must be some sort of standard, because, as Quirk points out, standards are necessary and people feel disoriented if there are none. While specialised subgroups of English users (doctors, lawyers) will have their own international ESP variety (regulated by the members of the in-group) the question arises what the model for general ELT in a given country should be. According to Kachru this problem can be solved in two ways: one can either use an exo-normative model, that is a native-speaker standard (usually British or American English), or an endo-normative model, that is the local educated norm.

Kachru distinguishes between three attitudinal stages regarding the acceptance of a local variety: in the first stage the localised form is not recognised. In the second stage the local form is extensively diffused. Finally, the educated localised norm is recognised by contextualising the teaching material to fit local socio-cultural situations, by recognising the intranational uses of English and by accepting local creative writing in English as part of the national writing. In the final stage, English may well be a link in culturally and linguistically pluralistic societies.

2.6. European Perspective

Today, "any European...who switches on the radio has a very

good chance of striking upon some popular music with an English-language text". Additionally, English is currently spread—or spreads itself—through film, TV, advertising and—perhaps most importantly in our technological age—software and the internet. As a consequence, English is today the most important source for loans in all European languages. Today 42% of European citizens claim to be able to converse in English. When it comes to language teaching, English is the language most widely taught in Europe. It comes therefore as no surprise that there is a significant generation-gap in English language proficiency.

Because of the marked differences between European countries it is reasonable to assume that the status of and the attitudes connected with English will vary considerably across Europe. In general, however, it is safe to assume that the function of English in Europe is "...not that of a popular vernacular, but of a necessary means of communication in certain well-defined situations".

In Western Europe English use into three parts:

- *Intense use of English:* The Netherlands, Luxembourg and the Scandinavian Countries.
- *Moderate use of English:* Germany, Switzerland, Austria, Belgium, France.
- *Little use of English:* The Mediterranean Countries (except in some tourist areas).

During communist times, English was seen as the language of freedom by many intellectuals in the East. When the iron curtain finally fell the demand for and the use of English in Eastern Europe exploded. The following reasons for the popularity of English come to mind:

- Because of ideological reasons English was neglected in education while Russian played a prominent role.
- The necessity of understanding English texts
- The usefulness of English if one wants to use the newly won freedom to travel to foreign countries.
- The rising demand for competence in English in key professions.

– The desire to comprehend English which one encounters in daily life.

As Philipson and Skutnabb-Kangas themselves point out, most East European countries have long-established national languages. Another factor is that in Eastern Europe there is a long history of foreign language learning built upon the principle that student and teacher have the same mother tongue. Hence Eastern European teachers are less eager to rely on authentic material and on a native-speaker teacher. Still, it seems that English is gaining ground in Eastern Europe, particularly among the young.

2.6.1. Scandinavian Countries and the Netherlands

Starting with the Scandinavian countries, it could be said that they have most successfully assimilated English. According to Phillipson the Danish minister of education even claimed that English is the second mother tongue of his country. This fits in with a ministerial note from 1978 which states that the official aim of ELT in Danish schools is to make the population bilingual. Code-switching is also common.

Similarly, Ferguson praises the high level of English language competence in Sweden. To some extent this may be because in Sweden films and radio-programmes are often shown in English only—even without subtitles. Therefore, Ljung's conclusion that English in Sweden is used by a surprisingly large percentage of people—not only for work but also in connection with leisure-time activities like watching television programmes in English—does not come as a surprise. Furthermore, a large number of Swedes also read in English.

In regard to the situation in the Netherlands, the impact of English may only be superficial, despite the fact that EFL already starts in primary school:

> Dutch knowledge of English is far more often passive than active, tuned towards understanding films and texts rather than producing the films and texts themselves...Dutch pop groups often perform in English but Dutch actors rarely do so and Dutch writers (naturally!) never do.

Although English plays an important role it has not been used for local purposes to the same extent as in former British colonies. All of the countries in this region are rather small speech communities; English is therefore often perceived as a "window to the world" which helps these countries to compete internationally. At the university, some subjects may even be taught in English. Generally, English is seen as an indicator of modernisation and is therefore frequently used in advertising.

2.6.2. France

English seems to be quite popular and widespread in France as Flaitz' analysis of movies, radio programmes and job advertisements shows. The fact that 85% of schoolchildren decided to learn English as a foreign language and, moreover, the fact that even the Ecole Central de Paris requires fluent English for all its graduates supports Kachru's argument that even those who have a critical attitude towards English see to it that their children learn the language. Thus even the French seem to admit—albeit somewhat grudgingly—that English is important in international communication.

Furthermore, in accord with the European trend, a generation gap seems to exist: while the older generation tends to know only French, the young primarily use English to communicate with other nationalities. Interestingly, Claude Truchot notes that the practice of using English in conversation, which was fashionable only in trendy circles ten years ago, has become more general. Even the effect of the language laws seems to be rather limited.

2.6.3. Italy and Spain

Italy provides a good example of a truly Mediterranean country. As in so many other European countries, it was post-war Americanisation through which English was spread. Italians borrowed a number of words from the fields of sport, music, entertainment, business and technical subjects. For Dardano English contributed substantially to a second Europeanisation of Italian. According to Pulcini

> the appeal of English words [to the Italians] is due not only to their cultural prestige, but...also to their structural features: their brevity and phonic effect..., their flexibility in word-formation...and their similarity to Italian words.

This brevity has, according to Dardano a connotation of modernity and efficiency—at least for some users. Today, Anglicisms seem to be accepted into the standard language at a rapid pace. Dardano emphasises that the influence of English is not only present in the upper classes, but is also felt at the middle and lower levels of the Italian linguistic community. The influx is particularly high in various technical sub-codes. Still, in schools English is only learned by 60 percent of the pupils. Interestingly, Pulcini notes a decline of the American myth in Italy and thinks that the growing acceptance of European unification may lead "to a shift of interest from English to other foreign languages".

The contemporary attitude towards English seems less marked by purism than in some other European countries; perhaps this liberalism is still a counter-movement to the extremely hostile reaction to foreign loans during the fascist period when various substitutions for Anglicisms were proposed. In Spain, as a contrast, attitudes towards English loans seem to be more critical. One purist even put the use of an Anglicism on a par with lack of morals and personal hygiene. Generally speaking, Anglicisms are introduced because one needs to lexicalise an object or a process. The advertising industry has exploited this fact and uses technical or pseudo-technical Anglicisms to increase the attractiveness of products. English is thus used for image-making.

2.6.4. Ireland

Ireland has been referred to as "England's first colony". The status of English in Ireland is in many ways more similar to (post)colonial Englishes than to English on the continent. Indeed, writers like Brian Friel have depicted English as the language of the coloniser. Gaelic, the official language of the country, is hardly spoken outside a small confined area (called the Gaeltacht) and this area is still shrinking. While pupils are compelled to learn Gaelic at school and while a knowledge of Gaelic is also a prerequisite for certain jobs, no one can force people to actively use the language. Particularly in the big cities the triumph of English has been overwhelming. In Northern Ireland, the varieties of English spoken "...distinguishes some Catholics from some Protestants as clearly as colour distinguishes an Afrikaner from a Zulu". Actually, this fact may be an indication of the extent that

English has become an Irish language. After all, some of the greatest "English" writers and poets were born in Ireland.

2.6.5. Austria and Germany

The spread of English in Austria and Germany, however, has been somewhat neglected (particularly in the anglophone areas) and therefore merits more extensive treatment. German and Austrian merchants who had trade connections with the British Isles certainly used English before the 18 century. In the middle of the century another motive for learning English arose: more and more people wanted to read English literature. Thus the English language profited from the general rise in literacy and the development of a literary culture in the German speaking areas.

Between 1770 and 1840 English was established as a school subject in Germany. Now adolescent learners began to learn English in great numbers. Whether English was offered and to which extent depended on the type of school: those schools which were more practically oriented and/or which were attended by the middle classes put more emphasis on English while the elitist Gymnasium with its emphasis on Latin and Greek remained sceptical for a long time. Those who wanted a place for English at the Gymnasium had to argue that modern languages had not only a practical but also an educational value.

In the multilingual Habsburg Empire, English faced competition from various native languages. Generally speaking, Austria introduced English much later than Germany: in 1778 the first effort to establish English at the University of Vienna had failed because the Empress Maria Theresia regarded the English language as dangerous for the morals of her citizens. However, only twenty-two years later attitudes had changed; knowledge of English was now seen as being of advantage to the student. Thus, a teacher of English was installed at the university. At Austrian state schools, however, Pazelt maintains, there was virtually no ELT before 1848. Interestingly, in 1908 the demand for an expansion of ELT at the university was already justified with the argument that English was of growing importance as an international medium of communication.

The influence of English also increased steadily outside the education system. Due to Britain's position as the workshop of the world the influx of loans intensified. In 1889 this development was harshly criticised by Herman Dummler at a congress of the newly found "Allgemeine Deutsche Sprachverein." Bismarck, when asked what he considered to be the decisive factor in modern history, replied "that the North Americans speak English". However, both in Austria and in Germany English remained the second foreign language behind French.

With the arrival of World War One German and Austrian society changed radically. Dummler's essay about the usefulness of EFL in wartime Germany is a fascinating case-study of how English was appropriated at the time. Dummler's main argument is the lingua franca use of the language. It is not, he argues, the superiority of German goods which is responsible for the success of the German trade industry but the German merchant's clever adaptability in the field of language—that is his ability to use English.

Dummler considers England Germany's arch enemy; hence English should be learnt because it can be used as a weapon against Britain. In fact, not learning English would only increase the enemy's position because without knowledge of English the German merchant would be easily ousted from international trade. With this background in mind it hardly comes as a surprise that Dummler rejects teaching pupils what London looks like and how to behave there. Rather, because it is closely related to German, English should be used to make them aware of the history of the German language. Within limits, Dummler thinks that English also encourages (logical) conceptual thinking. Generally, the children should learn about other cultures so that they are better able to evaluate their own. Dummler already exploits the ideological opportunities ELT provides: the pupils should be made aware of the fact that the first world war was a result of the British claim for world power.

Britain is portrayed as an oligarchy ruled by the landed gentry and is described as interfering in the affairs of other nations. Still, Dummler holds that the good sides of the English characters should be mentioned: he contrast English national pride favourably with German love of foreign things.

From 1934 to 1938 Dollfuß and Schuschnigg ruled autocratically in the Austrian "Ständestaat". In the Ständestaat, like in the Third Reich, education was seen as ideological indoctrination: the two pillars of Austrian education at the time were religious-ethical and nationalistic education. The emphasis on modern languages was increased: in Vienna the number of English courses was doubled. Modern Languages in general and English in particular were appropriated for several aims. Firstly, English was used as a means of selecting pupils "suitable" for higher education. Secondly, the teaching of foreign languages was meant to stress the European dimension of Austrian education and, implicitly, the European nature of the Austrian state itself. Furthermore, pupils should be made "fit for survival" by being able to work in tourism and trade.

In Austria, the whole school-system was radically changed when the Nazis took power in 1938. The only purpose of a whole section of the former Austrian ministry of education was to transfer the Austrian into the German system. In the new system the so-called "Oberschule" took 8 years with English as the first foreign language starting in the first form. Only in the 7 form was Latin added. This completely reversed the Ständestaat educational policy.

The end of Nazi rule led to a decrease of the prestige of the German language in Germany and Austria. Conversely, the Germans and Austrians became even more open to the (main) language of the Western Allies, English. Post-war philologists, however, did not deal critically with the Nazi period. Rather, it was the Americans who placed great emphasis on the denazification of education. While German had been the most important subject in NS education, in post-war Germany English played a leading role. The dominance of English as the first foreign language was thus not only retained but extended. The main differences between textbooks of the 50's and the 30's are:

— a pervasive renunciation of military topics and heroes.
— the abandonment of racial studies
— the relinquishing of nationalistic criticism of Great Britain

Post-War ELT textbooks, influenced by re-education, feature texts about democracy, religion, humanitarism and politics. The unity of European culture is also emphasised.

In post-war Austria the number of pupils learning English increased from 39.199 to 64.631. Conflicts arose between the American educational personnel who favoured contemporary children's literature and best-sellers and the native Austrian teachers who put emphasis on classical English literature. Thus the new ELT curriculum was a conglomerate of diverging educational policies which were simply added to the 1928 curriculum. Although it was ready by the academic year 1946/7 the curriculum was rejected by several provinces: in Voralberg the 1935 curriculum was used, Upper Austria used the 1928 curriculum and Carinthia and Styria a mixture of both. This resulted in a confusing mix of different types of schools in different provinces starting either with Latin, French or English as the first foreign language.

In everyday life the Austrians soon got accustomed to the foreign troops. In fact, as a cartoon in the magazine "Film" suggests, the Austrians became "Americanised" while the Americans, in turn, became "Viennised". One way in which this Americanisation process was aided by the US institutions was through the appropriation of ELT. For the pupils British English may well have been associated with formal education while the American variety was the one of leasure time communication with the new role-models, the GIs.

In tertiary education, exchange programmes enabled young scientists to go to the Unites States but also brought American visiting lecturers to Austria. Consequently, the number of lectures dealing with the US exploded: while only 50 courses had dealt with the US in the period from 1919 to 1945, in 1946 alone there were already more than 100.

The British both co-operated and competed with the Americans in the battle for the hearts and minds of the Austrians. Similar to the Americans, they donated books and installed guest lecturers at the university. The British Council organised a variety of cultural activities to convey the British way of life to the Austrians. Naturally, the British supported the intention of giving ELT a prominent place in Austrian education. However, they had far less money to their disposal than the Americans; hence their aim was to "re-educate the educators"; thus they concentrated on the elites rather than on the masses. Generally, by speaking English in post-war Austria one established a connection with the victors. The possibility to communicate with the Allied forces directly increased one's social status and prestige.

In contemporary Austria one can, generally speaking, encounter English in many domains, from business, advertising, or marketing to culture. There are two English language theatres, CNN and NBC Europe, some cinemas which show films in English and a range of English-language magazines. In 1979 a new radio station called "Blue Danube Radio", which broadcast only in English, was founded. Originally it was meant for employees of the new UNO-City in Vienna but it soon found a wider audience. Of course, the Americahouse and the the British Council also have a branch in Austria. The Austrian British Council issues the language teaching journal "ELT News" and offers the Cambridge Examinations. Other societies which aim at furthering relations between Austria and Great Britain or Austria and the USA are the Anglo-Austrian Society, the Austro-American Society and the Österreichisch-Britische Gesellschaft. Furthermore, in a pilot-project called "English Language Teaching across the Borders" (ELTAB) English was used as a bridge to Austria's eastern neighbours.

In the current system, English is already taught in primary school. At secondary schools English is an obligatory subject taught between 3 and 5 hours per week. The officially prescribed goals are that the pupils should be able to understand authentic written and spoken texts and learn to express themselves appropriately. However, communicative competence was never the sole objective. While the 1961 curriculum specified that EFL should also teach pupils objectivity, industriousness, distance and the recognition of authority nowadays modern languages are meant to promote tolerance of other cultures, to broaden the pupils. horizons and to contribute to the development of their personalities. It does not seem to me as if these aims are sufficiently realised in current Austrian ELT textbooks, though.

In many schools English can additionally be chosen as an optional subject. Recently, it has become fashionable to use English as a working language in projects at school, most often in combination with history and social studies but sometimes also in geography and economics. In 20% of the projects where English is the working language only English is spoken, in 60% German is used to translate technical terms. However, in most cases terms are only translated into German when the pupils indicate that they do not understand them. Abuja and Heindler recommend native speakers as teachers for such projects.

As EFL in state schools is often not sufficient for business life, the pupils of private or international schools may be in a favoured position regarding their job prospects. It is therefore little wonder that private lessons in English are a flourishing business. Even children in pre-schools and primary schools are sent to private institutions to improve their English because parents fear that they will not be able to compete otherwise.

Although the 1993 curriculum is remarkably liberal in its emphasis on the ability of making oneself understood in an international setting in practice the native speaker is still the model in a majority of cases.

2.7. Teaching English as an International Language (TEIL)

In today's multipolar world international English plays an important role and will continue to do so for the foreseeable future. Hence a paradigm shift from Anglo-Saxon centred ELT towards TEIL is urgently needed—both in general and in the Austrian education system in particular. Unfortunately, though, international English is currently rather disregarded, both in ELT at school and, perhaps even more disturbingly, at TESL/TESOL programmes as well as in teacher education.

References

Ammon, Ulrich, "The status of German and other Languages in the European Community", In: Coulmas, Florian (ed.) *A Language Policy for the European Community: Prospects and Quandaries*, Berlin.: De Gruyter, 1991.

Bailey, Richard W., *Images of English: a cultural History of the Language*, Cambridge: CUP, 1991.

Brann, Conrad M.B., "Lingua minor, franca & nationalis", In: Ammon, Ulrich (ed.) *Status and Function of Languages and Language Varieties*, Berlin: de Gruyter, 1989.

Crystal, David, *English as a global Language*, Cambridge: CUP, 1997.

Görlach, Manfred, "English as a World Language - the State of the Art", *English World Wide*, 1988.

Harmer, Jeremy, *The Practice of English Language Teaching*, New Edition, London: Longman, 1991.

3

Globalisation of English

Over the past two or three decades, English has come to occupy a singular position among languages. Previously only one among several dominant European languages, on a par with French or Spanish, it is today a *world* language, *the* language people use whenever they wish to communicate with others outside their own linguistic community. English has become the lingua franca of the global network: where the TCP/IP protocol secures technical communication between computers via the internet, English is the "protocol" for oral and written communication across national frontiers. As English has moved toward paramountcy, the status of the other principal languages has changed. Even though they are spoken by more people today than ever before, they have been demoted, degraded in relation to English.

Today, French, Spanish, Arabic, German, Russian, etc., more or less have the status of regional languages, national languages that can be used beyond their national frontiers. But, they are losing their currency as the language of international communication, formal and informal: both in political and commercial contexts and in intercultural exchanges, as bridges between people who cross cultural frontiers or who like to enrich their lives with media products from abroad.

The different languages have also been affected by the challenge English poses, tending to a greater or lesser degree to absorb English words, pronunciation, word order, and so forth. At the same time, a growing number of languages and dialects are in aanger of extinction. Linguists count approximately 6,800 different languages in the world today. The languages differ widely in terms of the number of people who use them. The eleven most widely used languages encompass nealy half the population of the planet. While not the most widely spoken language, English was spoken by about 341 million people as their first language in 1999. Roughly 500 million spoke English as their first or second language.

Some 417 languages are considered virtually extinct today; they are spoken by very few, elderly people. But many more languages have experienced decline in various respects. The trend is no new phenomenon, nor can it be attributed exclusively to the spread of English. In fact, the trend can be traced back centuries, during which time European imperialism over most of the planet contributed to the dominance of a handful of languages at the expense of a number of local languages and dialects. Linguistic imperialism has frequently followed in the wake of economic and political imperialism.

Linguistic homogenisation is not only a consequence of global imperial domination; the process of *nation-building* has also contributed. Frequently, the creation of nation-states has involved the adoption of a single national language, whereupon education and cultural expressions in other dialects and languages within the national frontiers have ceased. Not infrequently, use of subordinate languages and dialects has been forbidden or subject to political sanctions. In a similar fashion, different dialects of the designated national language occupy different positions in a rank order, where one dialect is the prescribed norm. Thus, globalisation and the predominance of English at the expense of other languages is nothing new. It is rather a question of a radicalisation and acceleration of a centuries-long trend, in which local varieties of language die out, and more universal varieties survive.

Globalisation has not, however, acted solely to homogenise language and promote use of English. And it also promote regional languages like Scots Gaelic, Welsh, Catalan and Kurdish. Most of these movements have not identified their adversary as globalisation per se, but rather the dominant language of the dominant national culture, like, for example, Turkish in Turkey. In some instances—in Norway, for example—the defense of dialects has been incorporated in national linguistic policy. There, mainstream media, too, are engaged in the effort to preserve both parochial dialects and the synthetic, dialect-based national language, New Norwegian. The political struggle for recognition of local and regional languages is part of a greater striving *for* cultural identity and recognition, and *against* the hegemony of the majority culture(s) of the nation-state. Viewed in this perspective, national linguistic cultures may be said to be under attack from without and within, which is very much in keeping with globalisation theorists' characterisation of the process as being at once globalising and localising.

3.1. English as a Global Language

There are 6,912 languages in use around the globe today. While this is less than in previous years, such a large number of languages make communication between people in different countries—or even in the same country in some cases—very difficult. There has been talk for years of a "global language" for the future, a single language to be used in place of the thousands spoken today. While the benefits of a global language seem obvious, in terms of ease of communication and business dealings, there are also potential negative effects, including the deaths of currently spoken languages and the alteration of cultures from forced outside influence. In addition, there is also the issue of which language would become global. Mandarin Chinese is spoken by almost 900 million people according to a 1998 census, almost three times as many who speak Spanish or English, which are the next two most commonly used languages with approximately 330 million speakers each. Perhaps Spanish or English might be better candidates since they are official languages in 20 and 51 countries, respectively, as opposed to only three countries claimed by Mandarin. There is also the option of using an artificial language such as Esperanto, designed as an international language with a structure and pronunciation key that allow for ease of learning and use.

In recent years, there has been a great increase in globalisation, or the sharing of ideas and information worldwide. Due to advances in communications technology, including the telephone networks and the Internet, a global language will be required in the future. This language may not be officially acknowledged, but even today several candidates for a global language are emerging.

Because of its presence in many countries around the globe and its entrenchment in science and technology, English is the best available candidate.

English is a Germanic language which has passed through three major stages in its history: Old English, Middle English, and Modern English. The first ancestor, Common Germanic, came into being approximately three thousand years ago in the Elbe river region and eventually split into three distinct subgroups. West Germanic invaders from Jutland and southern Denmark between 500 and 800 AD brought about the rise of Old English in the British Isles. As the invaders spread through the area, the Celts were pushed north and west, into Scotland and Ireland, but pieces of their languages remained behind to be incorporated into Old English. In 850, Norse invaders came to the shores and brought their own language, a derivative of North Germanic. Some of these words were also eventually incorporated into English. Although the majority of the words currently included in an English dictionary are originally from foreign languages, almost half of the most common words have roots in Old English.

English entered its second phase in 1086 when William the Conqueror, Duke of Normandy, conquered England. English became the language of the Anglo-Saxon peasants while the new nobility spoke Anglo-Norman, a variant of Old French. Although it also had Germanic influences, Anglo-Norman was a Romance language and brought back the influence of Latin to England. In some cases Anglo-Norman words replaced Anglo-Saxon, particularly in areas where the nobility ruled, such as the courts. In other areas, words from the two languages combined to form new words. For example "gentle" from French and "man" from Germanic become "gentleman." There were also times when words from both languages were used interchangeably, one of the reasons there are so many synonyms today. In the twelfth century, the French nobles who remained in England were becoming more estranged from their relatives back in their home country, and as their English holdings became more important they began to use a more modified version of English to communicate with their subjects. When the bubonic plague passed through England, about a third of the population was killed and the lower classes became more prominent, raising the use of English over Anglo-

Norman and contributing to the end of class differences in language use.

The language recognised as English today, Modern English, came into being during the Renaissance. This was the language of Shakespeare, and many Latin and Greek words were revived and introduced to the population of England. During the late 1400s the printing press was developed in England, bringing literacy to the masses and helping to standardise the language. The first English dictionary was published in 1604. Since then, the structure of the language has not changed a great deal, but the number of words included has greatly increased. This is due in part to the Industrial Revolution when Latin and Greek terms were often used to describe the wonders that were developed, and partially due to British colonialism. With portions of the Empire spread across the globe, words from many different languages were incorporated into English.

In the twentieth century, two world wars brought words from even more languages. Also, since the majority of the male populations of Britain and the United States served in the military, several military slang terms such as "ASAP," for "as soon as possible," also became common in everyday speech. American English was also influenced by many Native American languages, as well as Spanish and French from other colonial expansions and West African languages due to the slave trade.

English was not the only language that developed through the ages. Spain, France, and Portugal were developing their languages, also Germanic and Romance based, in the same time period and region. What gave English an advantage over these other languages was the military power of the British Empire. Although the phrase, *"El imperio en el que no se ponía el sol"* or "The empire on which the sun never sets" was used originally by Charles V to describe his Spanish empire, in the nineteenth century it applied far better to the British. Spanish is second only to English in the number of countries where it is an official language, but Britain truly had an empire that spanned the globe until the middle of the twentieth century.

At its peak, the British Empire covered almost a third of the world's surface and encompassed approximately a quarter of the world's population. When the British colonised portions of India and Africa as well as America, sent their convicts to Australia, and had military and colonial presence on various islands around the world as well, they took their language with them. While many of the native words influenced English, English also had an effect on the native speakers. Today, although there is no longer a British Empire, many of these places retain use of the English language. The United States, Canada, and Australia are three of the most obvious examples, although English is also considered an official or national language in Kenya, India, Singapore and many other countries. Today, although not technically "empires," with territories and military presences around the world, both Britain and the United States can claim the sun never sets on their citizens.

Another major cause of the rise of English as a possible global language has been access to knowledge. Between 1750 and 1900, about half of the major scientific and technical advancements came from Britain and the United States. These innovations greatly increased the amount of written material in English, particularly in the sciences which had previously had most publications done in French or Latin. Taking advantage of these advancements required an understanding of the English language. At the same time, international banking firms, such as those owned by J.P. Morgan in New York and the Rothschilds in London, were investing far more money in foreign trade than their counterparts. Since both primarily conducted their business in English, it gave the language a stronger foothold in the business world. The acceptance of English into the scientific and business communities was an important step in its development as an international language.

The spread of English has continued, and in recent years the number of people speaking English has increased even faster than it did at the turn of the twentieth century. This is due to increased globalisation, as technology makes travel and communication around the world much faster and more accessible than in previous years. Tourism and travel to foreign countries is becoming common, and being able to communicate upon arrival is convenient. Because English does have a presence around the world, it is often used for communication.

Three of the other main mediums for the transmission of the English language in the twentieth century were advertising, media broadcasting, and the Internet. Advertising is the oldest of the three mediums and actually started back in the Industrial Revolution with magazines such as *Cosmopolitan*. Publications were able to reduce selling prices and therefore attract more consumers by allowing advertising in their pages, and today two thirds of a newspaper might be devoted to ads. Other forms of advertising, such as posters and billboards, became common in the 1920s. Firms such as Ford and Coca-Cola became household names in this decade. As these products began to spread to the international community, English was carried with them. Today, even in countries where English does not have any recognised status, English advertisements are common.

Broadcasting started with radio when KDKA of Pittsburgh, Pennsylvania broadcast its first program in November, 1920. In Britain, the British Broadcasting Corporation was established in 1922, and in the next five years other broadcasting companies appeared in cities all over Europe as well as in places such as Bombay and Calcutta. Agreements over frequency usage were necessary, and while it makes sense that organisations such as the International Broadcast Institute would use English since it is based out of London, the only official language of the Asia-Pacific Broadcasting Union is also English. Nearly a third of all the radio broadcasts around the world were in English, and not all of these originated in countries where English was an officially recognised language. After World War II the number of English radio broadcasts increased, with new areas of coverage including the Soviet Union, Germany, and Italy.

Movie and television broadcasts also brought English to the rest of the world, since the majority of them were in fact in English. Although the movie industry actually began in England and France, World War I caused a great deal of disruption and the industry became centered in the United States, specifically Hollywood, California. When sound was added to films, English was the language broadcast. In 1996, 80% of all movies released were in English, and not only is the major awards ceremony, the Oscars, English-based, half of the awards given at the Cannes Film Festival in France are given to English-language films. Oftentimes the same movies showing in both Spain and Russia will be the same English film, either dubbed or with subtitles added. The fact that the actors and actresses in these movies are speaking primarily English is an important factor because, according to

David Crystal, an authority on the English language and author of *Cambridge Encyclopedia of Language* and *Cambridge Encyclopedia of the English Language*, "'People increasingly believe in what they see, and they buy what they believe in...People use, drive, wear, eat, see, and buy what they see in the movies.' If this is true, then the fact that most movies are made in the English language must surely be significant, at least in the long term".

The Internet, and computers in general, have been major proponents of the English language in recent years. In fact, ASCII, the display language of computers, uses single byte codes allowing for 2 possible characters. For languages requiring more characters or characters not supported by those eight bits, other means of translation have to be not only devised, but means of encoding and decoding must be available for translation on both ends. Messages in languages such as Chinese and Hindi often have to be transmitted as images or special libraries downloaded in order to view them.

Another technological factor giving English an advantage over many other languages is that computers were first developed in the United States. Computer keyboards only have character keys for the twenty-six letters of the English alphabet, the corresponding numbers, and various punctuation marks. While there have been keyboards designed for other languages, for example the Bicameral Pictographic Keyboard for Chinese, and the addition of diacritical markings for languages such as Spanish and French, these have been more recent developments and require specialised software to run. Companies such as Microsoft have foreign language plug-ins of their products, but these are often released after their English counterparts and do not always contain all of the same features. For example, while Microsoft Office can have its home language set to Russian, the spell check, grammar check, and thesaurus functions are no longer usable without the addition of more software. On the same note, many games released in the United States are put through only rough translation before being sent abroad. Many games developed internationally come into the United States after the same type of limited translation.

The Internet is seen in many countries as a way of gaining knowledge from around the world and providing opportunities in many different industries, including promoting tourism and crafts. However, on the Internet, over half of the available websites are in English. Although this is an approximate number since it is impossible to survey all websites in existence, the fact that the Internet was developed from the ARPANET in the 1970s in the United States meant that English speaking countries had an advantage from the start. According to Anatoly Voronov, a director of GlasNet in Moscow, "It is far easier for a Russian language speaker with a computer to download the works of Dostoyevsky translated into English to read than it is for him to get the original in his own language". This is slowly changing, but it is still common to see "also available in English" on foreign websites, making it likely that English will continue to be a formidable presence on the Internet. Although there are translation mechanisms available, human translation is costly and time-consuming, and machine translation on sites such as Free Translation are often incorrect since they simply translate the words rather than the meaning. This is the equivalent of picking up a foreign language dictionary and expecting to be able to speak fluently because all of the words are known. These translation programs also do not currently take into account words that exist in two languages and mean completely different things, or common idioms in any language, making them poor substitutes for real translation.

3.2. Influence of English on Danish Language

English has influenced the Danish language, as it has many other languages, throughout the latter half of the twentieth century. The influence is noticeable in pronunciation, declensions and conjugations, as well as word order, but the most obvious influence is the number of new words having their roots in Anglo-American culture.

The influence of English on the Danish language is only one facet of Anglo-Saxon influence. Today, increasingly, there are settings in Denmark in which English has supplanted Danish. Some large corporations having extensive operations and contacts abroad have introduced English as the company language; some fields of science, where Danish and/or several foreign languages were once used, have converted to English. Information technology, music and music publishing, and advertising are other branches where English is rapidly gaining ground, in some instances to the exclusion of Danish. Linguists characterise the situation as a "loss of domain", and it is precisely losses of domain that worry some Danish researchers most. Danish as such will surely survive, but losses of domain may reduce Danish in terms of both extent and status. If Danish is on the ebb in key areas of life in Denmark—not least in fields having to do with new technologies and so-called growth sectors—its vitality and versatility may be at risk.

If Danish is becoming more and more receptive to influences from English, it is at the same time becoming less receptive to local varieties of Danish. Danish dialects have receded steadily throughout the period of Denmark's modernisation, starting in the nine-teenth century, and today we find hardly any true dialects left. Generally speaking, regional dialects are spoken mostly by elderly people and people with less formal education, whereas young people and more highly educated individuals tend to speak standard Danish. Meanwhile, new linguistic varieties that are specific to uses of new media—chatrooms, text messages, e-mail etc.—have emerged. These are characterised by a mixture of formal and informal styles and new combinations of spoken and written forms.

Mass media are often singled out as the most important factors behind the increasing influence of English on Danish. Generally, the frequency of English in media content is simply taken as a sort of index of the degree of influence without any further discussion of the role of the media in the process. Preisler has probed deepest into the relationship between English and Danish in conjunction with his study of mediated subcultures. He tends toward the view that the media themselves are not responsible for the influence. According to Preisler, the prime factors are to be found in overall changes in Danish culture. Danish society is undergoing a general Anglo-Americanisation, and it is here we find the causes of linguistic influences. In Preisler's view, the media mirror culture rather than create it. But the issue of media influences on Danish hardly originated with the advent of globalisation. Media have played a role in linguistic rivalries and power struggles for centuries, and when we consider linguistic influences in a historical perspective, it becomes clear that they are social and cultural phenomena and not simply a question of establishing a common national language with standardised diction.

Standard Danish, the norm now challenged by English and miscellaneous medialects, is no natural or even impartial version of the Danish language; it is the dialect that emerged victorious out of a cultural and social power struggle. A historical perspective also reveals the roles foreign influences on Danish have played in the articulation of social and cultural hierarchies in the country. There have been periods when losses of domain to one or another foreign language were much more far-reaching than either the situation today or what is likely to obtain in the foreseeable future.

Thus, "standard Danish," the language virtually all Danes speak today, is the product of a very long social and cultural process, the aim of which has been the establishment of a unified national culture. Standard Danish is the linguistic result of a nation-building project, whereby nation-state and society were to be forged into one, where state, people, culture and language were linked together through the construction of a common Danish identity. In the course of the process, elites had to relinquish their ties with other linguistic cultures, while commoners were made to sacrifice their local idiom. Standard Danish became the common denominator, the basis for the homogenisation of Danish society within the framework of the welfare state. It is the language in which all Danes could feel at home in a modern, industrialised and urbanised Denmark. Given globalisation, the bond between nation-state and people is no longer fully so unequivocal. In an increasing number of contexts, "Danishness" is neither self-evident nor adequate as a framework for social interaction and identity-formation. Whether in the business world, in politics, or the Arts, Danishness is under stress. Danishness can no longer serve as the common denominator of state and society when both state and society have been globalised.

Media influence the Danish language in several ways. In addition to overall anglicisation, there are usages that are specific to activities and situations where different media are involved. These media-specific usages, *medialects,* are a consequence of the circumstance that a steadily growing share of human communication takes place via media. New media are constantly appearing on the scene, and they influence all kinds of communication, from the strictly private to the totally public: cellphones, text messages, e-mail, chatrooms, and so forth. Media are increasingly present *in* the language as an infrastructure, through which we communicate with one another. This observation raises at least two points that have bearing on the influence English exerts. First, English is the linguistic vehicle for meta-communication about mediated communication. Second, the increasing mediatisation of communication affords considerable leeway for linguistic innovation and creativity. While the media contribute to a narrowing of the spectrum of foreign languages to English, they also provide the preconditions for linguistic differentiation and innovation.

As new forms of mediated communication continue to arise, a meta-language attached to each medium develops that users of the medium use to steer the conduct of the communication. It may consist of technical terms that describe specific choices of operating systems, web addresses, browser types, etc.; verbs and nouns that denote actions and situations that are part of the communication; use of abbreviations that arise because of the verbal limitations of the medium, and, finally, popular expressions/slang for the activity itself, e.g., to text, to chat, to mail, etc. Inasmuch as nearly all new media in the twentieth century were developed and first launched in Anglo-American settings, and since the software industry, too, is dominated by Anglo-American companies, these meta-languages generally have English roots. In time, domestic equivalents may develop. In many countries, however, only some of the words will be translated; in Denmark translations are few and far between. Thus, every new medium has been and will likely continue to be accompanied by a wave or ripple of English influence. English has become the meta-language that enables the conduct of communication.

At the same time, new media constitute a material resource for new forms of communication, and thanks to them we can note a good deal of linguistic innovation and creativity in connection with their emergence. Another principal linguistic characteristic that is common to media old and new is the change in the relationship between formal and informal forms of expression.

Like dialects and sociolects, medialects are assigned ranking in social and cultural status hierarchies, and they are inclusive and exclusive, defining social groupings, large and small. Mastery of a given medialect confers status in the act of communication, just as those who lack a command of the medialect either feel excluded or are repulsed by the particular mode of communication.

3.2.1. New Localities of Globalisation

Under the influence of globalisation, media contribute in some ways to standardisation of the Danish language, and to linguistic variety and creativity in others. On the one hand, the media spread English, often at the expense of other languages. In this sense the media are a homogenising factor. On the other hand, the media have considerable potential for a new kind of linguistic diversity that transcends the various national languages in that innovation is attached to use of the media, not the individual user. In this sense, the media are a differentiating factor. Globalisation may be seen as a new epoch in linguistic history. The "golden age" of dialects was associated with an essentially rural society, where agricultural production was the norm and industrial production was still in its cradle, a society where the local community was central and permanence the rule, where mobility across geographical and other boundaries was the exception. With the advent of industrial production, urbanisation and national consciousness, dialects were forced to retreat before the onslaught of a standardised national language. In Denmark, the battles between the dialects and standard Danish reflected conflicts between town and country, between province and capital, between the farm and the factory. The global network society, finally, impacts on the social hierarchies of national industrial society. Not least its valuation of mobility means that a command of English and modern communications technologies confers status.

The global society is a mediated society, where communication via electronic networks constitutes a new reality. The ability to take part in these networks has more than symbolic importance; increasingly it has implications for individuals' economic standing, job opportunities and success on the marketplace, cultural identity and sense of belonging in society. The media are the places where people now meet, trade, provide services, converse and present themselves to one another. English and the medialects may thus be seen as the dialects of globalisation. Geographical place is losing its importance, being supplanted by electronic, virtual localities—and, as this occurs, local varieties of language are supplanted by global varieties of language like English and the medialects.

References

David Wilton, "A (Very) Brief History of the English Language", 3 Sept. 2005.

David Crystal, *English as a Global Language,* Cambridge University Press, Cambridge, UK, 2006.

David Rohde, "Do You Speak American?", *Global American,* 2003.

Paul Johnson, "Must the Whole World Speak English?" Forbes.com, 29 Nov. 2004.

Raymond G. Gordon, Jr. (ed.), *Ethnologue: Languages of the World,* 15 Edition, SIL th International, Dallas, Tex., 2005.

Roland J. and L. Breton, "Can English Be Dethroned?" *UNESCO Courier,* April 2000.

4

English as a Global Language

A language achieves a genuinely global status when it develops a special role that is recognised in every country. This might seem like stating the obvious, but it is not, for the notion of 'special role' has many facets. Such a role will be most evident in countries where large numbers of the people speak the language as a mother tongue—in the case of English, this would mean the USA, Canada, Britain, Ireland, Australia, New Zealand, South Africa, several Caribbean countries and a sprinkling of other territories. However, no language has ever been spoken by a mother-tongue majority in more than a few countries, so mother-tongue use by itself cannot give a language global status. To achieve such a status, a language has to be taken up by other countries around the world. They must decide to give it a special place within their communities, even though they may have few (or no) mother-tongue speakers.

There are two main ways in which this can be done.

Firstly, a language can be made the official language of a country, to be used as a medium of communication in such domains as government, the law courts, the media, and the educational system. To get on in these societies, it is essential to master the official language as early in life as possible. Such a language is often described as a 'second language', because it is seen as a complement to a personas mother tongue, or 'first language'. The role of an official language is today best illustrated by English, which now has some kind of special status in over seventy countries, such as Ghana, Nigeria, India, Singapore and Vanuatu. This is far more than the status achieved by any other language—though French, German, Spanish, Russian, and Arabic are among those which have also developed a considerable official use. New political decisions on the matter continue to be made: for example, Rwanda gave English official status in 1996.

Secondly, a language can be made a priority in a country's foreign-language teaching, even though this language has no official status. It becomes the language which children are most likely to be taught when they arrive in school, and the one most available to adults who—for whatever reason—never learned it, or learned it badly, in their early educational years. Russian, for example, held privileged status for many years among the countries of the former Soviet Union. Mandarin Chinese continues to play an important role in South-east Asia. English is now the language most widely taught as a foreign language—in over 100 countries, such as China, Russia, Germany, Spain, Egypt and Brazil—and in most of these countries it is emerging as the chief foreign language to be encountered in schools, often displacing another language in the process. In 1996, for example, English replaced French as the chief foreign language in schools in Algeria.

In reflecting on these observations, it is important to note that there are several ways in which a language can be official. It may be the sole official language of a country, or it may share this status with other languages. And it may have a 'semi-official' status, being used only in certain domains, or taking second place to other languages while still performing certain official roles. Many countries formally acknowledge a language's status in their constitution (e.g. India); some make no special mention of it (e.g. Britain). In certain countries, the question of whether the special status should be legally recognised is a source of considerable controversy—notably, in the USA. Similarly, there is great variation in the reasons for choosing a particular language as a favoured foreign language: they include historical tradition, political expediency, and the desire for commercial, cultural or technological contact. Also, even when chosen, the 'presence' of the language can vary greatly, depending on the extent to which a government or foreign-aid agency is prepared to give adequate financial support to a language-teaching policy.

In a well-supported environment, resources will be devoted to helping people have access to the language and learn it, through the media, libraries, schools, and institutes of higher education. There will be an increase in the number and quality of teachers able to teach the language. Books, tapes, computers, telecommunication systems and all kinds of teaching materials will be increasingly available. In many countries, however, lack of government support, or a shortage of foreign aid, has hindered the achievement of language-teaching goals.

Distinctions such as those between 'first', 'second' and 'foreign' language status are useful, but we must be careful not to give them a simplistic interpretation. In particular, it is important to avoid interpreting the distinction between 'second' and 'foreign' language use as a difference in fluency or ability. Although we might expect people from a country where English has some sort of official status to be more competent in the language than those where it has none, simply on grounds of greater exposure, it turns out that this is not always so.

4.1. Why a Language becomes a Global Language

Why a language becomes a global language has little to do with the number of people who speak it. It is much more to do with who those speakers are. Latin became an international language throughout the Roman Empire, but this was not because the Romans were more numerous than the peoples they subjugated. They were simply more powerful. And later, when Roman military power declined, Latin remained for a millennium as the international language of education, thanks to a different sort of power –the ecclesiastical power of Roman Catholicism. There is the closest of links between language dominance and economic, technological, and cultural power, too, and this relationship will become increasingly clear as the history of English is told. Without a strong power-base, of whatever kind, no language can make progress as an international medium of communication. Language has no independent existence, living in some sort of mystical space apart from the people who speak it. Language exists only in the brains and mouths and ears and hands and eyes of its users. When they succeed, on the international stage, their language succeeds. When they fail, their language fails.

This point may seem obvious, but it needs to be made at the outset, because over the years many popular and misleading beliefs have grown up about why a language should become internationally successful. It is quite common to hear people claim that a language is a paragon, on account of its perceived aesthetic qualities, clarity of expression, literary power, or religious standing. Hebrew, Greek, Latin, Arabic and French are among those which at various times have been lauded in such terms, and English is no exception. It is often suggested, for example, that there must be something inherently beautiful or logical about the structure of English, in order to explain why it is now so widely used.

Latin was once a major international language, despite its many inflectional endings and gender differences. French, too, has been such a language, despite its nouns being masculine or feminine; and so—at different times and places—have the heavily inflected Greek, Arabic, Spanish and Russian. Ease of learning has nothing to do with it. Children of all cultures learn to talk over more or less the same period of time, regardless of the differences in the grammar of their languages. And as for the notion that English has 'no grammar'—a claim that is risible to anyone who has ever had to learn it as a foreign language—the point can be dismissed by a glance at any of the large twentieth-century reference grammars.

This is not to deny that a language may have certain properties which make it internationally appealing. For example, learners sometimes comment on the 'familiarity' of English vocabulary, deriving from the way English has over the centuries borrowed thousands of new words from the languages with which it has been in contact. The 'welcome' given to foreign vocabulary places English in contrast to some languages (notably, French) which have tried to keep it out, and gives it a cosmopolitan character which many see as an advantage for a global language. From a lexical point of view, English is in fact far more a Romance than a Germanic language. And there have been comments made about other structural aspects, too, such as the absence in English grammar of a system of coding social class differences, which can make the language appear more 'democratic' to those who speak a language (e.g. Javanese) that does express an intricate system of class relationships. But these supposed traits of appeal are incidental, and need to be weighed against linguistic features which would seem to be internationally much less desirable—notably, in the case of English, the accumulated irregularities of its spelling system.

A language does not become a global language because of its intrinsic structural properties, or because of the size of its vocabulary, or because it has been a vehicle of a great literature in the past, or because it was once associated with a great culture or religion. These are all factors which can motivate someone to learn a language, of course, but none of them alone, or in combination, can ensure a language's world spread. Indeed, such factors cannot even guarantee survival as a living language –as is clear from the case of Latin, learned today as a classical language by only a scholarly and religious few. Correspondingly, inconvenient structural properties (such as awkward spelling) do not stop a language achieving international status either.

But international language dominance is not solely the result of military might. It may take a militarily powerful nation to establish a language, but it takes an economically powerful one to maintain and expand it. This has always been the case, but it became a particularly critical factor in the nineteenth and twentieth centuries, with economic developments beginning to operate on a global scale, supported by the new communication technologies –telegraph, telephone, radio—and fostering the emergence of massive multinational organisations. The growth of competitive industry and business brought an explosion of international marketing and advertising. The power of the press reached unprecedented levels, soon to be surpassed by the broadcasting media, with their ability to cross national boundaries with electromagnetic ease. Technology, chiefly in the form of movies and records, fuelled new mass entertainment industries which had a worldwide impact. The drive to make progress in science and technology fostered an international intellectual and research environment which gave scholarship and further education a high profile.

Any language at the centre of such an explosion of international activity would suddenly have found itself with a global status. By the beginning of the nineteenth century, Britain had become the world's leading industrial and trading country. By the end of the century, the population of the USA (then approaching 100 million) was larger than that of any of the countries of western Europe, and its economy was the most productive and the fastest growing in the world. British apolitical imperialism had sent English around the globe, during the nineteenth century, so that it was a language 'on which the sun never sets'.

4.2. Global English

The world has seen quite a few international languages in the past, but not anything like English. The uniqueness of English as an international language is not merely a matter of scale. Global English is a distinct and new phenomenon with a dynamism and a logic of its own. What we need today is an adequate theory of Global English.

Global English is not merely a descriptive term, it is a theoretical construct as well. A failure to recognise this has in fact resulted in distortions in our perceptions of its manifestations. Recent history of language studies shows that we made an analogous mistake in be in g tardy in recognising that a second language variety is not a deviant form of a first language variety but in certain important ways a manifestation of a distinct theoretical construct. There are indications that a similar mistake is being made in the case of Global English.

There are different perceptions about English in India. Some have been hostile to it because they tend to regard it primarily as a remnant of a foreign imposition, a vestige of our colonial past, and as a language which has usurped the rightful place of indigenous languages and their literatures. It has been looked upon with favour by those who regard it primarily as a valuable means of promoting the commercial, economic, technological and industrial interests of the country in the modern world. A few have seen it as an immense cultural asset, as our window not only on world science but also on world culture. There is, however, another equally important dimension of English: English is a valuable resource for India not only because it opens to us the magnificent countries of the mind but also because it renders possible to us the most magnificent expression of our own soul. Some Indians have felt that India needs English to express her inmost individuality which, they feel, cannot be expressed through any other language.

English is probably the first language in recent human history to have ever been accepted 'from within', so widely. This acceptance from within by people of diverse linguistic backgrounds and from different parts of the world is an important feature of a World language. Nothing illustrates this inward acceptance of English better than the case for Indian writing in English made nearly 50 years ago by K. D. Sethna. Sethna points out how English because of the extraordinary crop of poets in English history is not only unquestionably the most highly developed of modern languages but also how English has come to surpass all modern languages, including those of India herself, in acquiring the immediacies and intimacies of intuitive speech and thus become a language best suited to express the 'true soul' of India. Sethna was careful to recognise that not every Indian would have either the gift or the urge for using the English language for creative self-expression. But he declared that to maintain that Indian writing in English can only be an exotic curiosity and never an organic unfolding of genuine Indianness is to indulge in a sweeping superficiality.

Until the middle of the 19th century, French was a greater international language than English. Today the influence of French has diminished outside the franco—phone countries while English is gaining everywhere. There certainly are a host of reasons to which English owes its ascendancy today. But one of these reasons is probably that the teaching of impeccable, native, French was an explicit policy of French governments while the British have been more tolerant in this respect and have taken a more or less neutral attitude towards the emergence of different national English accents. World English will no doubt continue this tradition. This latitude that English has so far enjoyed in developing according to the individualities of the different communities which use it is one of the necessary conditions for the growth of a Global Language.

Chinese is probably the right model for Global English. Chinese dialects are intelligible outside the dialect boundary only in the written form but are not always intelligible across this divide in the spoken form. Similarly Global English does not have to aim at every speaker of its innumerable varieties being intelligible to all other speakers of the language in the spoken as well as the written medium. If you consider the global scope of English, this would seem to be totally impracticable. As it is, many of the varieties of Indian English are not intelligible to speakers of many varieties of British or American English or even to speakers of ESL varieties such as Nigerian English. But global communication through English does not mean that each individual who learns English has to have this competence. When English is taught more or less as a compulsory subject at school to literally scores of millions of students, the aim of this teaching cannot be attaining international intelligibility in the spoken form. English will have to be content to aim at such international intelligibility primarily at the receptive level and that too in the written variety.

A Global Language unites people because it enables each linguistic community which uses it to feel at home within its fold. The function of a Global Language is to foster an international or global consciousness without suppressing diversity in its manifestation. English needs to be liberated from the restrictions we still seem to impose on it because we do not always seem to be able to remember that it is a new linguistic phenomenon.

4.3. Reasons for English Became a Global Language

How does a language become global? Well the first obvious thing is that long ago people needed to communicate with each other in order to trade, in order to exchange goods. So one reason for the globalisation of a language is trade. If you can't communicate with each other it's very difficult to buy and sell goods and exchange goods. The second reason why a language may become global is conquest. Conquest, well what does that mean? Conquest is defeating, taking control of other countries by military means. In other words sending your army into another country in order to control it and suppress it. The reasons for conquest are many. Sometimes it is just that the leader of a particular country is power-crazy, and wants to control more and more countries. Or there might be long standing bad feeling between countries which then leads to a war. It might be for religious reasons, it may be for geographical reasons, it may be because of natural disaster. There are all sorts of reasons why countries go to war with each other. But anyway the most powerful country will usually invade and control the weaker countries.

The third reason why a language may become global is migration. People moving from one country to another *en masse*, in a large number. Another factor is what we call 'expansion diffusion'. So as people migrate or as people invade a country, they bring the language with them that they speak, and they pass this language on to local people. Now this may result in various things, different dialects, the development of new words, in the language. The adoption of words from the language where the main, the global speakers have moved, so for example English people invaded India during the 18th century and as a result of that they brought English to India. India started to use English. Indian people started to use English, but a lot of Indian words got adopted into the English language. Words like 'bungalow' which is like a small house, a one-storey house. It is an Indian word, which is now part of the English language. So as the English language expanded, as this global language expanded, words from other countries which they expanded to were brought into English. There are many, many examples.

Of course another very very important reason why a language becomes global, is because of the introduction of new channels of communication. TV is the most obvious one in information technology, the internet, and such. But before that, there were other things. You know there was the telephone, the telegraph, you know. These days everybody sends the emails. But 20 years ago, 25 years ago, 30 years ago, everybody sent telegrams if they wanted to send a message. They went down to the post office and sent a telegram. All of these are things which can impact on the growth of a language and make it global.

There are 1,400 million people where English has official status. These are the people who use English as an official language although they may not be using English in their everyday language at home. In fact there are 1.3 billion people currently learning English as a second or foreign language. So in this room at the moment there are about 22, 23 people learning English. You are part of 1.3 billion, according to the British Council website which was most recently updated in 2005, last year. Almost 2 billion speakers, English speakers world wide. In other words one, oh that's wrong it should be 1 out of 3 people, I in 3 people is speaking English, is using English. 1 in 3, so whoever said 80% slightly exaggerated. You said 1.5 billion, that's about 25%, it's actually about 33% so you were not far off.

Well Chinese has the most number of first language speakers but English has the most number of official language speakers. So

Chinese/English, English/Chinese, they feature very prominently in both these tables. As does Hindi, the language, most common language in India, notice also Spanish has an important position as well. And this is for historical reasons before the great expansion of England, of the English speaking people, before that, came a great expansion of Spanish speaking people, now you probably know from your own knowledge that the Spanish colonised the whole of South America, apart from Brazil. So, all those countries in South America became, use Spanish as their official language, and all the people you meet from South America are Spanish speaking. In fact, in South America, Spanish has had a far greater influence on every person, than English has had, for example, in Africa. Because if you go to Africa, although English is your official language in many of those countries, especially Southern and Eastern Africa, at home most of the people speak their own local language. But if you go to South America, most people at home will speak Spanish.

Eminent linguist called Braj Kachru who developed three circles of English. This model very briefly talk about, how English has developed as a global language. And he talks of the inner circle which is the country's using English as a native language. Then the outer circle which are countries using English as an official language. Recognising the importance of English as an international language, so Braj Kachru, over 20 years ago now, developed this model.

4.3.1. Historical Reasons

Moving on, we have looked at why English became a global language, and now just let's look at the historical reasons why English became a global language. The first is the pioneering voyages. If you look at your map, you see the United Kingdom, this little area here, is on the edge of Europe. They had the greatest sea power in the world.

In 1588, the English navy defeated the Spanish navy, the famous Spanish navy called the Armada. This defeat was—the British fleet was lead by the man called Sir Francis Drake—who came from not far away from here in town called Plymouth. Well, not that far away. And he defeated the Spanish Armada and this was very significant because the only rival sea power in the world at that time were the Spanish. And Sir Francis Drake, and subsequent famous seamen, British seamen, including Captain Thomas Cook, began a series of voyages all over the world in their ships. Voyages of exploration to explore, to find out more about the world. They had very small ships, ships which were not much bigger than three times of the size of this room. So if you take this wall here, and you think of walking all the way to the far side of the building, that's about as far as big as the ship would be. They used to take the ships all around the world. You've seen the movies, yeah? And it was the British seamen, that were particularly successful, these were called Pioneers. To pioneer is to do the, to be the first, if you are pioneer, you are the first person to do something. So these were pioneering voyages. That was one reason, one historical reason why English became a great, a major global language.

The second one was colonialism. There was a demand for raw materials by British manufacturers, and there was demand to, expand the Empire; it became a tradition in Britain. And as a result, many countries in the world were colonised. You know, you know, for example that South Africa, most of Southern Africa, India, Sri Lanka, many countries were colonised by the British, parts of Asia as well, Malaysia, for example. Many parts of that.

In the 19th century, Britain was the first country really to undergo an industrial revolution. This was brought about by the age of steam. The invention of the steam locomotive and steam-driven engines in Britain, meant the development, before any other country, of modern industry. The demand for modern industry was raw materials, and raw materials could only be found often in countries far away. So those countries were colonised by the British naval power and military power in order to get raw materials. And of course the English language went with this trade, so the industrial was something that encouraged the development of trade, the development of military conquest, and the spread of English. During the 19th century Britain and many other European countries were engaged in conflict.

At the beginning of the 20th century, Britain and many other countries became engaged in a major war—the First World War. So that their energy was concentrated on these wars. America in the meantime developed. The United States developed quietly, almost, while the rest of the world was at war with Germany, and

France and Britain, and Austria, Turkey, they were all involved in a huge world war. At the right time the Americans came into the war on the side of the British and the French, and defeated the Germans. And this gave them two things. Great economic superiority because they had not been wasting their economic effort on war, they'd been developing industry. And because they came in at the last minute and saved the day for the British and the Allies, the French, the Belgians and the other countries on the British side, they had great political influence with those countries. And those countries had been victorious in the war. So America had, during this time of war in Europe, had developed economic superiority and political leadership. But of course the thing was, in America, English was a *lingua franca,* the language that was spoken.

So American superiority, and the fact that English is the official language of the United States, contributed to the development of English as a global language. And then finally, of course there was American technological superiority. During the 20th century this world presence was maintained and promoted almost singlehandedly through the economic superiority or supremacy of the new American super power. And the language behind the US dollar was English.

For more than half a century, immigrants from the Indian subcontinent and the West Indies have added variety and diversity to the rich patchwork of accents and dialects spoken in the UK. British colonisers originally exported the language to all four corners of the globe and migration in the 1950s brought altered forms of English back to these shores. Since that time, especially in urban areas, speakers of Asian and Caribbean descent have blended their mother tongue speech patterns with existing local dialects producing wonderful new varieties of English, such as London Jamaican or Bradford Asian English. Standard British English has also been enriched by an explosion of new terms, such as *balti* and *bhangra.*

4.4. Ways to Speak English

As with the Anglo-Saxon and Norman settlers of centuries past, the languages spoken by today's ethnic communities have begun to have an impact on the everyday spoken English of other communities. For instance, many young people, regardless of their ethnic background, now use the black slang terms, *nang* ('cool,') and *diss* ('insult' – from '*disrespecting*') or words derived from Hindi and Urdu, such as *chuddies* ('underpants') or *desi* ('typically Asian'). Many also use the all-purpose tag-question, *innit* – as in statements such as *you're weird, innit*. This feature has been variously ascribed to the British Caribbean community or the British Asian community, although it is also part of a more native British tradition–in dialects in the West Country and Wales, for instance – which might explain why it appears to have spread so rapidly among young speakers everywhere.

4.4.1. Influences from Overseas

The English Language can be traced back to the mixture of Anglo-Saxon dialects that came to these shores 1500 years ago. Since then it has been played with, altered and transported around the world in many different forms. The language we now recognise as English first became the dominant language in Great Britain during the Middle Ages, and in Ireland during the eighteenth and nineteenth centuries. From there it has been exported in the mouths of colonists and settlers to all four corners of the globe. 'International English', 'World English' or 'Global English' are terms used to describe a type of 'General English' that has, over the course of the twentieth century, become a worldwide means of communication.

4.4.2. American English

The first permanent English-speaking colony was established in North America in the early 1600s. The Americans soon developed a form of English that differed in a number of ways from the language spoken back in The British Isles. In some cases older forms were retained – the way most Americans pronounce the <r> sound after a vowel in words like *start, north, nurse* and *letter* is probably very similar to pronunciation in 17th century England. Similarly, the distinction between past tense *got* and past participle *gotten* still exists in American English but has been lost in most dialects of the UK.

But the Americans also invented many new words to describe landscapes, wildlife, vegetation, food and lifestyles. Different pronunciations of existing words emerged as new settlers arrived from various parts of the UK and established settlements scattered along the East Coast and further inland. After the USA achieved independence from Great Britain in 1776 any sense of who 'owned' and set the 'correct rules' for the English Language became increasingly blurred. Different forces operating in the UK and in the USA influenced the emerging concept of a Standard English.

4.4.3. Influence of Empire

Meanwhile, elsewhere, the British Empire was expanding dramatically, and during the 1700s British English established footholds in parts of Africa, in India, Australia and New Zealand. The colonisation process in these countries varied. In Australia and New Zealand, European settlers quickly outnumbered the indigenous population and so English was established as the dominant language. In India and Africa, however, centuries of colonial rule saw English imposed as an administrative language, spoken as a mother tongue by colonial settlers from the UK, but in most cases as a second language by the local population.

4.4.4. English around the World

Like American English, English in Australia, New Zealand and South Africa has evolved such that they are distinct from British English. However, cultural and political ties have meant that until relatively recently British English has acted as the benchmark for representing 'standardised' English – spelling tends to adhere to British English conventions, for instance. Elsewhere in Africa and on the Indian subcontinent, English is still used as an official language in several countries, even though these countries are independent of British rule. However, English remains very much a second language for most people, used in administration, education and government and as a means of communicating between speakers of diverse languages. As with most of the Commonwealth, British English is the model on which, for instance, Indian English or Nigerian English is based. In the Caribbean and especially in Canada, however, historical links with the UK compete with geographical, cultural and economic ties with the USA, so that some aspects of the local varieties of English follow British norms and others reflect US usage.

4.5. Becoming the Dominant Global Language

English is also hugely important as an international language and plays an important part even in countries where the UK has historically had little influence. It is learnt as the principal foreign language in most schools in Western Europe. It is also an essential part of the curriculum in far-flung places like Japan and South Korea, and is increasingly seen as desirable by millions of speakers in China. Prior to WWII, most teaching of English as a foreign language used British English as its model, and textbooks and other educational resources were produced here in the UK for use overseas. This reflected the UK's cultural dominance and its perceived 'ownership' of the English Language. Since 1945, however, the increasing economic power of the USA and its unrivalled influence in popular culture has meant that American English has become the reference point for learners of English in places like Japan and even to a certain extent in some European countries. British English remains the model in most Commonwealth countries where English is learnt as a second language. However, as the history of English has shown, this situation may not last indefinitely. The increasing commercial and economic power of countries like India, for instance, might mean that Indian English will one day begin to have an impact beyond its own borders.

English is well on its way to becoming the dominant global language. But the global dominance of the English language is bad news for world literature, according to CEPR researcher Jacques Mélitz (Centre de Recherche en Economie et Statistique, Paris and CEPR). Because if the English language dominates world publishing, very few translations except those from English to other languages will be commercially viable. As a result, virtually only those writing in English will have a chance of reaching a world audience and achieving 'classic status'. The outcome is clear, Mélitz argues: just as in the sciences, those who wish to reach a world audience will write in English. "World literature will be an English literature", Mélitz warns, "and will be the poorer for it—as if all music were written only for the cello". His work appears in "*English-Language Dominance, Literature and Welfare,*". By literature, he refers to imaginative works of an earlier vintage that are still read today, and therefore the accumulation of world literature refers to the tiny fraction of currently produced imaginative works which will eventually be regarded as 'classics'. According to Mélitz, the tendency of competitive forces in the global publishing market to privilege the translation of English fiction and poetry into other languages for reading or listening enjoyment may damage the production of world literature and in this respect make us all worse off.

Mélitz makes the following points:

— *Language matters:* In the case of literature, as opposed to other uses of language, language does not serve merely to communicate content (say, a story line) but is itself an essential source of enjoyment. Therefore, it is futile to argue that nothing would change if all potential contributors to literature wrote in the same language. "We might as well pretend that there would be no loss if all musical composers wrote for the cello" said Mélitz. Translations can only approximate the rhythms, sounds, images, allusions and evocations of the original, and in literature, those aspects are essential.

— *Great authors write in only one language:* Remarkably few people have ever made contributions to world literature in more than one language. Beckett and Nabokov may be the only two prominent examples. Conrad, who is sometimes mentioned in this connection, is a false illustration in a glaring regard: he never wrote in his native Polish. Quite conspicuously, expatriate authors generally continue to write in their native language even after living for decades away from home. This holds not only for poets, such as Mickiewicz and Milosz, which may not be surprising, but also for novelists. Mann went on composing in German during a long spell in the US.

— *English is much more likely to be translated:* For straightforward economic reasons, only works that enjoy exceptionally large sales have any notable prospect of translation. Heavy sales in the original language represent an essential criterion of selection for translation, though not the only one. As a result, translations will be concentrated in original creations in the major languages. Since English is the predominant language in the publishing industry, authors writing in English have a much better chance of translation than those writing in other tongues.

— *English dominance of translations has increased:* The dominance of English in translations has actually gone up over the last 30 years, despite a general decline in the market share of English in the world publishing market. When English represented about a quarter of the world publishing market in the early 1960's, the percentage of English in translations was already 40%. With the general advance of literacy and standards of living in the world, the share of English in world publishing fell to around 17% in the late 1980's. Yet the language's share in translations rose to surpass 50% during this time.

— *If you want to reach a world audience, write in English:* In science, as in literature, a person writing in a minor language has a better chance of publication than one writing in a major tongue, but will necessarily have a much smaller chance of translation and international recognition. The result in science is clear. Those who strive to make a mark in their discipline try to publish in English. By and large, the ones who stick to their home language—English excepted, of course—have lower ambitions and do less significant work. The same pressure to publish in English exists for those engaged in imaginative writing who wish to attain a world audience.

— *English dominance may cause the world pool of talent to dry up:* However, the evidence shows that in the case of literary writing, the gifted—even the supremely gifted—in a language other than English generally cannot turn to English by mere dint of effort and will-power. Thus, the dominance of English may sap their incentive to invest in personal skills and to shoot for excellence. Working toward the same result are the relatively easier conditions of publication they face at home. If so, the dominance of English in translations may cause the world pool of talent to dry up.

— *Literature may become just another field where the best work is in English:* In other words, the dominance of English poses the danger that literary output will become just another

> field where the best work is done in English. In this case, the production of imaginative prose and poetry in other languages may be relegated to the same provincial status that such writing already has acquired in some other areas of intellectual activity. But whereas the resulting damage is contestable in fields where language serves essentially for communication, such as science in general, the identical prospect is alarming in the case of literature.

One important argument in favour of English as a global language is its effectiveness. Chinese has more native speakers, however, it also has simplistic grammar, and it lacks articles, prepositions, verb conjugation and tense, singularity and plurality of nouns making it less effective than English at expressing complex meanings. It is also tonal, which limits the speaker's use of tone for emotional and conceptual expression. Furthermore most Westerners find the Chinese writing system difficult to grasp, whereas the Chinese and other groups tend to learn the Roman alphabet easily. The Roman alphabet is already the most widely used alphabet in the world today, and is shared by many disparate and seemingly unrelated languages, such as English (which has Germanic and French roots) and Spanish (which derives from the Vulgar Latin.) Since the Roman alphabet is phonetic (representing sounds) rather than character based (representing concepts) it is a more effective method of describing the actual sounds of words and phrases.

References

Cheshire Jenny (ed.), *English Around the World: Sociolinguistic Perspectives*, Cambridge University Press, 1991.

Iyengar K. R. S., *Indian Writing in English*, Sterling Publishers Pvt. Ltd., New Delhi, 1985.

Nadkarni M. V., "English in Mother Tongue Medium Education", *CIEFL Bulletin*, 1983.

5
English as Lingua Franca

The English language has unmistakably achieved status as the world's lingua franca through globalisation. English is now the official or dominant language for two billion people in at least 75 countries. According to the British Council, speakers of English as a second language probably outnumber those who speak it as a first language, and around 750 million people are believed to speak English as a foreign language. English is the most common language to communicate scientific, technological, academic, and international trade information. English is clearly the world's lingua franca, but how did it get that way? Part of the reason is the feedback loop driving its history—a dynamic which may serve to illustrate how globalisation often is the result of a natural course of events: before English infiltrated the world, many of the world's languages infiltrated English.

The term "lingua franca" originated in Mediterranean ports in the Middle Ages among traders of different language backgrounds. In order to carry on the business of trade, they spoke a common "patchwork" language consisting of bits of Italian mixed with Greek, French, Spanish, and Arabic words. Some of those words are still part of ordinary conversation today—in modern English. Nearly every language on Earth has contributed to the development of English. Languages of the Indian subcontinent provided words such as pundit, shampoo, pajamas, and juggernaut. From the Spanish are several words that came to define the spirit of the American "wild west:" mustang, canyon, ranch, stampede, and vigilante are a few examples. English has adopted literally hundreds of words from Arabic and Persian. Though some filtered down through other languages, these words that evoke images from American culture have Arabic origins:

tariff, sugar, hazard, jar, almanac, shrub, alcove, alfalfa, syrup, and spinach. Long is the list of words and expressions that came to English from "foreign languages."

Now with mass media, contemporary English slings its patchwork of historically adopted words and new pop slang back at the world in a very big way. Some say, too big a way. John Swales describes English as "Tyrannosaurus Rex" let loose in the world to gobble up other languages and, thus, their cultures. The Kenyan writer Ngugi wa Thiong'o has observed that the erosion of a first language results in the loss of understanding the corresponding culture: "Language carries culture, and culture carries . . . the entire body of values by which we perceive ourselves and our place in the world." Anne Pakir ultimately dubbed English a "killer language" when attempts to teach English alongside the first languages of her homeland Singapore only resulted in the rise of a new language: Singlish.

On the other side of the debate, Salman Rushdie says that creating new Englishes such as 'Singlish' can be a therapeutic act of resistance against whatever dominance English exerts upon a given culture. "To conquer English may be to complete the process of making ourselves free." Juliane House, professor of applied linguistics at Hamburg University, Germany, notes that the spread of English can actually enhance the preservation of local dialects. "Paradox as this may seem, the very spread of English can motivate speakers of other languages to insist on their own local language for identification, for binding them emotionally to their own cultural and historical tradition. There is no need to set up an old-fashioned dichotomy between local languages and English as the 'hegemonic aggressor': there is a place for both, because they fulfill different functions. To deny this is to uphold outdated concepts of monolingual societies and individuals."

It is the "different functions" aspect of English vs. 'other languages' that is fiercely debated today. The speaking of English often functions as an elevated socio-economic currency on the international market and in international diplomacy, while local languages are pressured to be kept within the home or within communities, or for entertaining tourists. English is the official language of the European Central Bank even though the bank is in Frankfurt, Germany, and no predominantly English-speaking country is a member of the European Monetary Union. English has become a commodity.

Globalisation of the IT marketplace is accelerating the effect of English as a commodity. For decades English has dominated the IT industry, from research and development, to the design of hardware and software. In 2002, there were signs that the impact of China's interest in respecting international intellectual property rights heralded a new era of China-led technology standards which would slow down the monopoly of technologies made primarily for English speakers. A new culture of IT researchers had developed in China which was not built on U.S.-trained engineers. However, more recently, India, which once was very concerned about China's enthusiasm for changing standards in the IT industry, now sees the threat as fading—partly due to Indian businesses assuming that China will take a long time to catch up in English language proficiency, and India's dominance of the outsourcing industry which was won in large part because of their command of the English language.

English, like so many other aspects of Western culture, has the potential to bring people together, or the power to divide people into classified groups. As the debate goes on, English will continue to grow and change with the same force that has always driven the patchworking of language: the natural desire to exchange goods and ideas.

5.1. Global Language and Culture

With international mass media and the internet we now have a chance to know what is going on in each corner of the world, while on the other hand we may actually know less about what is going on in our own local environment. Global accessibility is not necessarily synonymous with global communication. A big part of the potential users of global products/documentation may either not have access to global mass media or modern technology, or they may not speak English, or both. In these cases we notice that for the product/documentation to be truly global it must communicate in the languages and cultures of its users. This can also be seen in the growing businesses of internationalisation, localisation, and translation. For various reasons localisation and translation are not always the best option for getting global. Therefore sometimes the product/documentation is not localised/ translated at all, and sometimes the English version is shipped everywhere.

Sometimes translation and localisation are done only into the major cultures and languages, while smaller cultures and languages are left to cope with one of these major languages, most often English. In any case, English has truly become the commonly accepted *lingua franca* for global communication. It is often used in communication not only when translation does not take place, but it is also used as the source language for translation. Although in the global community today it may be easier to understand (or at least be aware of) other cultures and their communication strategies, it is hard to hide one's own cultural background.

Understanding culture is something which may be easily handled too superficially in the global marketplace. Although we all understand that there is no such thing as a global culture for all 6 billion of us and that we need to be aware of other cultures, we may think that subcultures of, for example, internet users, science, mass media, or technical communication are mostly global. We may also feel that since English is used in global mass media and modern technology, it would be understood by everyone in the same way. Although people may have a shared understanding of subcultures on one level, on a deeper level it is very difficult to prevent one's national culture from affecting oneself, also within a subculture. Not all technical communicators around the world agree on what is a good instructional text and a good document.

Language is the visible surface level of culture, but has its roots deep in culture. For this reason it is not possible to discuss the role of English only in terms of whether we should use U.S. or British English in global communication, or what level of language skill you need to be able to communicate in English. These things are on the surface level of culture, but they do not define how successful communication is in a global environment. More important than how the message is constructed, is often *why* it is constructed the way it is and whether it actually makes communication in the global environment successful.

The first and obvious level where culture manifests itself in texts and communication is the surface level: what is visible in the text itself and especially the vocabulary used. What needs to be taken into consideration in the communication event from this level are, for example, false friends, product names, words with different associative fields (pasta does not mean the same thing for Italians and Finns), terminology, abbreviations, acronyms, idiomatic expressions, slang, words with multiple meanings, and so on. Translators deal a lot with this level of cultural features.

The second level of culture manifests itself in the structures and communication strategies of the text, and these things need to be considered especially in localisation. The contents is affected by what people are used to, what they assume, what they recognise, graphics, gestures, colours, etc. Meanings of symbols, for example, vary between cultures: a skull and crossbones symbol means death in Western countries but not in Iraq; in Finland and North America an owl symbolises wisdom whereas in South America it is a symbol of witchcraft. These things limit the way you can use examples and metaphors in the text. There are also concepts which can be understood "correctly" only within one culture: holidays, seasons, national emblems, national monuments, national sports, as well as issues from the physical world such as are doors opened in or out of a building, what size some typical objects such as milk cartons are, or do you drive on the right or left side of the road.

Attitudes towards the structure of the text and stylistic issues such as the length of sentences are also on this level. For example, in some languages simplicity is appreciated, while in others simple equals "childish" or "unprofessional". In some languages simple language conveys unprofessional image (Germany) while some cultures and languages appreciate verbosity (Arabic). Some languages tend to avoid repetition (Italian), in some you need to repeat your main point throughout the text, and so on. In technical communication, for practical reasons simplicity is the norm, and this may not be the preferred approach for some cultures.

The third level of culture needs to be taken into consideration already in product/document design, approach, and strategy. It has to do with the sender's and recipient's cultural "mental programming". Geert Hofstede's well known study lists such things as power distance, individualism/collectivism, masculinity/femininity (genders and gender roles), uncertainty avoidance, and long-term orientation. Other such strategies are how to show authority, is it more important to be "cool" or to be strictly professional, what are typical every day situations, how do people work or learn, what is polite, or what do people look like.

You also have to take into consideration what the physical conditions of the use of the product or document are. For example, if the product is created in a culture where everyone can afford it, what if in the target culture a group of users can only afford one product and it will be used by many people, or the people in the target culture prefer using it together. The strategy for using the product can change dramatically. Hofstede says that of all the nations he studied, America is highest on the value of individualism. This finding is consistent with the complaint of non-American users of American packaged programmes that they presuppose "solitary problem solvers".

Kenneth Keniston tells a good example on this. A North-American educational software suite was adopted for use in some elementary schools in Argentina. Although well localised from a technical point of view, it did not reflect "Argentine realities". In part, this referred to the fact that an educational programme developed in one of the southern United States could not mirror the Argentine geophysical and human realities. Educators also complained that the software was "too individualistic": for example, it presupposed that each student would sit alone solving problems as efficiently as possible, rather than collaborating with other students, which was the preferred mode of problem-solving in the local primary schools. Both the set-up of the hardware and the software militated against a "more Argentine" solution.

When communicating in a language (English) which is known to people in other cultures, the surface level of culture, i.e. language itself is fairly easy to understand and has been widely discussed, for example, in translation theory. The second level is the level of localisation and internationalisation: what has to be taken into consideration when making the product, to anticipate the cultural "traps". Products and documents can probably be made fairly neutral on these levels, not perfectly suitable for any culture in particular and at the same time suitable for all of them. The third level which is most deeply embedded in culture is the most difficult to take into consideration in global products.

Depending on the culture there may be different assumptions on how the product will be used, what the reader wants to know first, how much assistance the reader needs, whether the reader wishes to use the documentation at all, whether the user wishes to read the document first or whether they wish to browse the document while they try out the product and so on.

Communication does not take place in a vacuum. There are always two ends: the sender and the recipient. For communication to succeed the recipient has to understand the message. It does not, in fact, matter so much if the message is "bad" if the recipient understands it correctly. If we think of the complex nature of how culture is manifested in texts, the task may seem impossible. In global communication we cannot cater for everyone's cultural needs. However, we must not forget that even though the cultural knowledge of the sender or the recipient would not be sufficient as such, the communication event can still be successful and often is.

Even though the sender would not have managed to localise the text to the target culture or make the text neutral, the recipient is usually very willing to make all effort needed to understand the message. Imagination and the ability to be able to put oneself to the shoes of someone in another culture plays a significant role in this, just as long as the sender has not completely managed to ignore trying to keep the text free of cultural strategies of the source culture, or does not make the recipient not want to make the effort by insulting the recipient in some way.

Even though educated about other cultures, what the recipients cannot improve immediately is their language skill. When people from different cultures use the same language, the sender of the message has the responsibility for the communication event to succeed. If the sender's language skills are better than the recipient's, the sender must make sure the message is not constructed in language which is too difficult to the recipient, or based on cultural models of clearly one specific culture. This does not mean that we should write documents that any person can read with two months of language training.

However, the reality is that when you know English well enough you should also be able to simplify it, but if your English is not good, there is no way you can improve it just for the sake of understanding a message.

The English language skills of the recipient do not even have to be "bad" for the communication to fail. We can see, people with very good English skills getting lost in an index and documentation just because they used the "wrong" word for searching information and when it failed they could not think of any synonyms, or they thought of other synonyms than the author had thought of. The words and synonyms do no even have to be complicated. For example, "adding", "creating", and "defining" or even "modifying" can be used synonymously, depending on what point of view the author has taken.

If the recipient does not understand the message, it does not matter how elaborate the language used in the message is. Sometimes good language skills can even hinder communication. And whenever possible you need to use navigational aids such as indexes or searches, and use the same strategies in them as well. These are things that all technical communicators probably learn in their education, but we should also think about who we are making these choices for and what do we base our choices on: do we think of people with our cultural mental models and language skills, or possibly people with completely different mental models and language skills. Therefore learning about culture is an important part of education for technical communicators, and anyone who needs to communicate in the global community.

5.2. Politics of Global English

In some cultures not using the English version of a product/ documentation is a political choice, and in that case it is feasible for the seller to comply to the requirements of the buyer and offer them what they want. In Japan, for example, a few years ago there was a recommendation that English be taught in all Japanese elementary schools. This ignited a debate over the role of American culture in Japanese life. Some teachers, parents, and students applauded the early development of proficiency in English, but not everyone agreed. Some argued that accepting English is tantamount to accepting the rule of the stronger, and warned that "global English language mass media like CNN and the Englishdominated Internet help spread the U.S. way of thinking, adversely affecting Japanese culture and tradition.".

On the other hand, English as a global language is the mother tongue in influential nations, a (second) language with official status in other countries, and a priority in foreign language teaching in other countries. For example, in Finland almost 100 % of students select English as their first foreign language and study it starting from the age of nine. With this in mind it may also be a political choice *not* to translate. It may, for example, be considered better for children to be taught to use programmes and documents that use English or some other widely used international language. Knowing these languages would, quoting Kenneth Keniston "equip students to enter the modern, multinational electronic world as full participants. To be entirely educated in local languages—whatever its merits in terms of national pride and identity—could produce a generation of students disqualified for work and participation in the most vital sectors of the international economy and culture."

Another point of view could also be that as English is in such a dominant role these days, those who speak English as second language may actually have an advantage over those who speak it as their first language and may never need to learn another language. Those with English as their second language know at least two languages, and, perhaps, by learning the language of another culture, also gain a wider understanding of other cultures and are this way better equipped not only to use two or more languages, but also to understand communication strategies of other cultures and global communication.

References

Bruthiaux, Paul, "Squaring the Circles: Issues in Modeling English Worldwide", *International Journal of Applied Linguistics,* 2003.

Décsy, Gyula, "Europe's Linguistic Future: The Eurish-Problem", *Eurasian Studies Yearbook,* 1993.

Gnutzmann, Claus, "'Standard English' and 'World Standard English', Linguistic and Pedagogical Considerations", *The Globalisation of English and the English Language Classroom,* Eds Claus Gnutzmann and Frauke Intemann. Tübingen: Narr, 2005.

House, Juliane, "Developing Pragmatic Competence in English as a Lingua Franca", *Lingua Franca Communication,* Eds Karlfried Knapp and Christiane Meierkord, Frankfurt: Peter Lang, 2002.

James, Allan, "English as a European *Lingua Franca*: Current Realities and Existing Dichotomies", *English in Europe, The Acquisition of a Third Language,* Eds Jasone Cenoz and Ulrike Jessner, Clevedon: Multilingual Matters, 2000.

______________, "The Challenges of the Lingua Franca: English in the World and Types of Variety", *The Globalisation of English and the English Language Classroom,* Eds Claus Gnutzmann and Frauke Intemann, Tübingen: Narr., 2005.

Jamal, Shabaz, "Kurds Demand English", *Iraqi Crisis Report No. 73,* 13-July-2004, Institute for War & Peace Reporting, London, 2004.

Phillipson, Robert, "Global English and Local Language Policies", *Language Problems and Language Planning,* Volume 25, Number 1, Spring 2001.

6

International English

International English is the concept of the English language as a global means of communication in numerous dialects, and also the movement towards an international standard for the language. It is also referred to as Global English, World English, Common English, or General English.

The modern concept of International English does not exist in isolation, but is the product of centuries of development of the English language. The English language evolved from a set of West Germanic dialects spoken by the Angles, Saxons, and, who arrived from the Continent in the 5th Century. Those dialects came to be known as Englisc, the language today referred to as Anglo-Saxon or Old English. English is thus more closely related to West Frisian than to any other modern language, although less than a quarter of the vocabulary of Modern English is shared with West Frisian or other West Germanic languages because of extensive borrowings from Norse, Norman French, Latin, and other languages. It was during the Viking invasions of the Anglo-Saxon period that Old English was influenced by contact with Norse, a group of North Germanic dialects spoken by the Vikings, who came to control a large region in the North of England known as the Danelaw.

Vocabulary items entering English from Norse are thus attributable to the on-again-off-again Viking occupation of Northern England during the centuries prior to the Norman Conquest. Soon after the Norman Conquest of 1066, the Englisc language ceased being a literary language and was replaced by Norman French as the written language of England. During the Norman Period, English absorbed a significant component of French vocabulary With this new vocabulary, additional vocabulary borrowed from Latin, a simplified grammar, and use of the orthographic conventions of French instead of Old English orthography, the language became Middle English. The "difficulty" of English as a written language thus began in the High Middle Ages, when French orthographic conventions were used to spell a language whose original, more suitable orthography had been forgotten after centuries of nonuse. During the late medieval period, King Henry V of England ordered the use of the English of his day in proceedings before him and before the government bureaucracies. That led to the development of Chancery English, a standardised form used in the government bureaucracy.

The emergence of English as a language of Wales results from the incorporation of Wales into England and also dates from approximately this time period. Soon afterward, the development of printing by Caxton and others accelerated the development of a standardised form of English. Following a change in vowel pronunciation that marks the transition of English from the medieval to the Renaissance period, the language of the Chancery and Caxton became Early Modern English and with relatively moderate changes eventually developed into the English language of today. Scots, as spoken in the lowlands and along the east coast of Scotland, developed independently from Modern English and is based on the Northern dialects of Anglo-Saxon, particularly Northumbrian, which also serve as the basis of Northern English dialects such as those of Yorkshire and Newcastle upon Tyne. Northumbria was within the Danelaw and therefore experienced greater influence from Norse than did the Southern dialects. As the political influence of London grew, the Chancery version of the language developed into a written standard across Great Britain, further progressing in the modern period as Scotland became united with England as a result of the Acts of Union of 1707.

There have been two introductions of English to Ireland, a medieval introduction that led to the development of the now-extinct Yola dialect and a modern introduction in which Hibernian English largely replaced Irish as the most widely spoken language during the 19th Century, following the Act of Union of 1800. Received Pronunciation (RP) is generally viewed as a 19th Century development and is not reflected in North American English dialects, which are based on 18th Century English.

The establishment of the first permanent English-speaking colony in North America in 1607 was a major step towards the globalisation of the language. British English was only partially standardised when the American colonies were established. Isolated from each other by the Atlantic Ocean, the dialects in England and the colonies began evolving independently. In the 19th century, the standardisation of British English was more settled than it had been in the previous century, and this relatively well-established English was brought to Africa, Asia and Oceania. It developed both as the language of English-speaking settlers from Britain and Ireland, and as the administrative language imposed on speakers of other languages in the various parts of the British Empire. The first form can be seen in New Zealand English, and the latter in Indian English. In Europe English received a more central role particularly since 1919, when the Treaty of Versailles was composed not only in French, the common language of diplomacy at the time, but also in English.

The English-speaking regions of Canada and the Caribbean are caught between historical connections with the UK and the Commonwealth, and geographical and economic connections with the U.S. In some things, and more formally, they tend to follow British standards, whereas in others they follow the U.S. standard.

6.1. Proponents of International English

International English proponents face on the one hand the belief that English already is a world language (and as such, nothing needs to be done to promote it further) and, on the other, the belief that an international language would inherently need to be a constructed one. In such an environment, at least four basic approaches have been proposed or employed toward the further expansion or consolidation of International English, some in contrast with, and others in opposition to, methods used to advance constructed international auxiliary languages.

1. *Laissez-faire approach.* This approach is taken either out of ignorance of the other approaches or out of a belief that

English will more quickly (or with fewer objections) become a more fully international language without any specific global legislation.

2. *Institutional sponsorship and grass-roots promotion of language programs.* Some governments have promoted the spread of the English language through sponsorship of English language programs abroad, without any attempt to gain formal international endorsement, as have grass-roots individuals and organisations supporting English (whether through instruction, marketing, etc.).
3. *National legislation.* This approach encourages countries to enshrine English as having at least some kind of official status, in the belief that this would further its spread and could include more countries over time.
4. *International legislation.* This approach involves promotion of the future holding of a binding international convention to formally agree upon an official international auxiliary language which would then be taught in all schools around the world, beginning at the primary level. While this approach allows for the possibility of an alternative to English being chosen, the approach also allows for the eventuality that English would be chosen by a sufficient majority of the proposed convention's delegates so as to put international opinion and law behind the language and thus to consolidate it as a full official world language.

English as an additional language (EAL) usually is based on the standards of either American English or British English. English as an international language (EIL) is EAL with emphasis on learning different major dialect forms; in particular, it aims to equip students with the linguistic tools to communicate internationally. Roger Nunn considers different types of competence in relation to the teaching of English as an International Language, arguing that linguistic competence has yet to be adequately addressed in recent considerations of EIL.

6.1.1. Universality and Flexibility

International English sometimes refers to English as it is actually being used and developed in the world; as a language owned not just by native speakers, but by all those who come to use it.

Basically, it covers the English language at large, often (but not always or necessarily) implicitly seen as standard. It is certainly also commonly used in connection with the acquisition, use, and study of English as the world's lingua franca ('TEIL: Teaching English as an International Language'), and especially when the language is considered as a whole in contrast with British English, American English, South African English, and the like. It especially means English words and phrases generally understood throughout the English-speaking world as opposed to localisms. The importance of non-native English language skills can be recognised behind the long-standing joke that the international language of science and technology is broken English.

6.1.2. Neutrality

International English reaches towards cultural neutrality. This has a practical use:

> "What could be better than a type of English that saves you from having to re-edit publications for individual regional markets! Teachers and learners of English as a second language also find it an attractive idea — both often concerned that their English should be neutral, without American or British or Canadian or Australian colouring. Any regional variety of English has a set of political, social and cultural connotations attached to it, even the so-called 'standard' forms." — Peters.

According to this viewpoint, International English is a concept of English that minimises the aspects defined by either the colonial imperialism of Victorian Britain or the so-called "cultural imperialism" of the 20th century United States. While British colonialism laid the foundation for English over much of the world, International English is a product of an emerging world culture, very much attributable to the influence of the United States as well, but conceptually based on a far greater degree of cross-talk and linguistic transculturation, which tends to mitigate both U.S. influence and British colonial influence. The development of International English often centers around academic and scientific communities, where formal English usage is prevalent, and creative use of the language is at a minimum. This formal International English allows entry into Western culture as a whole and Western cultural values in general.

6.1.3. Opposition

The continued growth of the English language itself is seen by many as a kind of cultural imperialism, whether it is English in one form or English in two slightly different forms. Robert Phillipson argues against the possibility of such neutrality in his Linguistic Imperialism. Learners who wish to use purportedly correct English are in fact faced with the dual standard of American English and British English, and other less known standard Englishes.

Edward Trimnell, author of *Why You Need a Foreign Language & How to Learn One* argues that the international version of English is only adequate for communicating basic ideas. For complex discussions and business/technical situations, English is not an adequate communication tool for non-native speakers of the language. Trimnell also asserts that native English-speakers have become "dependent on the language skills of others" by placing their faith in international English.

6.1.4. Appropriation Theory

There are also some who reject both linguistic imperialism and David Crystal's theory of the neutrality of English. They argue that the phenomenon of the global spread of English is better understood in the framework of appropriation, that is, English used for local purposes around the world. Demonstrators in non-English speaking countries often use signs in English to convey their demands to TV-audiences around the globe, for instance.

6.1.5. Many Englishes

There are many difficult choices that have to be made if there is to be further standardisation of Engiish in the future. These include the choice over whether to adopt a current standard, or move towards a more neutral, but artificial one. A true International English might supplant both current American and British English as a variety of English for international communication, leaving these as local dialects, or would rise from a merger of General American and standard British English with admixture of other varieties of English and would generally replace all these varieties of English.

This is the situation long faced by many users of English who possess a 'non-standard' dialect of English as their birth tongue but have also learned to write a more standard dialect. Many academics often publish material in journals requiring different varieties of English and change style and spellings as necessary without great difficulty. As far as spelling is concerned, the differences between American and British usage became noticeable due to the first influential lexicographers on each side of the Atlantic. Spelling is but a small part of the differences between dialects of English, and may not even reflect dialect differences at all (except in phonetically spelled dialogue). International English refers to much more than an agreed spelling pattern.

6.1.6. Dual Standard

Two approaches to International English are the individualistic and inclusive approach and the new dialect approach.

The individualistic approach gives control to individual authors to write and spell as they wish (within purported standard conventions) and to accept the validity of differences. *The Longman Grammar of Spoken and Written English*, published in 1999, is a descriptive study of both American and British English in which each chapter follows individual spelling conventions according to the preference of the main editor of that chapter.

The new dialect approach appears in *The Cambridge Guide to English Usage* which attempts to avoid any language bias and accordingly uses an idiosyncratic international spelling system of mixed American and British forms.

6.2. English is an International Language (EIL)

'International English' can be read as shorthand for 'English as an international language' (EIL). The longer term is, however, though more unwieldy, more precise because it highlights the international use of English rather than suggesting, wrongly, that there is one clearly distinguishable, unitary variety called 'International English'. McKay, in her book entitled *Teaching*

English as an International Language, also makes use of the shorthand term and defines it like this:

> International English is used by native speakers of English and bilingual users of English for cross-cultural communication. International English can be used both in a local sense between speakers of diverse cultures and languages within one country and in a global sense between speakers from different countries.

EIL has recently been introduced: *World English.* This is a very striking and innovative denomination, and it goes hand in hand with a striking and innovative treatment of the topic in that it takes significant steps towards a much more powerful and comprehensive account of EIL than has hitherto been available. Brutt-Griffler identifies "four central features of the development of global language":

(1) Econocultural functions of the language; [i.e., World English is the product of the development of a world market and global developments in the fields of science, technology, culture and the media]

(2) The transcendence of the role of an elite *lingua franca;* [i.e., World English is learned by people at various levels of society, not just by the socio-economic elite]

(3) The stabilisation of bilingualism through the coexistence of world language with other languages in bilingual/ multilingual contexts; [i.e., World English tends to establish itself alongside local languages rather than replacing them, and so contributes to multilingualism rather than jeopardise it]

(4) Language change via the processes of world language convergence and world language divergence [i.e., World English spreads due to the fact that many people learn it rather than by speakers of English migrating to other areas; thus two processes happen concurrently: new varieties are created and unity in the world language is maintained]

In a nutshell, Brutt-Griffler demonstrates that English owes its global spread as much to the struggle *against* imperialism as to imperialism itself. What needs to be emphasized in the present context, however, is that in Brutt-Griffler's account, bi- or plurilingualism is an intrinsic design feature of World English. She provides a carefully researched and well-argued basis for acknowledging the active role of EIL users as *agents* in its spread and in its linguistic development: they are not just at the receiving end, but contribute to the shaping of the language and the functions it fulfils. This is a perspective with very considerable implications for educational questions concerning the conceptualisation of English in European curricula.

6.3. International Issues of EIL

Whatever happens in the long term, EIL as the product of a world market and other global developments will be a *fait accompli* for some time to come –estimates concerning the future significance of English (i.e. its econocultural functions in the world) vary, but a general consensus seems to be emerging that sees its position fairly securely established for the next 50 years or so. It therefore has to be assumed that the demand for 'English' in schooling will remain strong in the foreseeable future –and indeed, English is being learned by people at various levels of society, not just by the socio-economic elite. If the position of English, on a global scale, is recognised for what it predominantly is, namely EIL, it follows that EIL is likely to establish itself alongside local languages rather than replace them, and to be shaped by all its users. This expectation is, of course, also strengthened by research into bi-and plurilingualism, which shows that if different languages fulfil different roles in societies, if they function differentially in various domains, different attitudes develop *vis-à-vis* the different languages involved, and different allegiances to these languages are formed. As a consequence, bi or plurilingualism tends to get stabilised in such sociolinguistic situations.

Sociolinguistic research indicates that if – and this is a vital condition – English is appropriated by its users in such a way as to serve its unique function as EIL, it does not constitute a threat to other languages but, precisely because of its delimited role and distinct status, leaves other languages intact. Properly conceptualised as EIL, 'English' can be positioned, quite literally, *hors concours*. EIL needs to be considered for European curricula, as an alternative option to ENL in some contexts and as the default option in others. There seem to be at least four relevant ways of considering EIL:

- *functionally:* the role of English in the world. This is generally acknowledged as a fact, welcomed by some and deplored by others.
- *conceptually:* this concerns people's perspective on and attitudes towards this global role of English; the question here is whether ways of thinking about English have kept pace with the rapid development in the functions of the language, whether concepts in people's heads have changed as the role of English in the world has changed.
- *linguistically:* an (open) empirical question – what does EIL actually look like and sound like? How is it spoken and written? Are there salient linguistic features which can be said to characterise EIL (perhaps regionally, e.g. in Europe)?
- *pedagogically:* an (open) educational question – what would/could teaching EIL actually mean, and how would it differ from teaching English as a foreign language or English as a second language?

Generally speaking, the state of discussion regarding these four perspectives on EIL is the following:

- *Functionally:* EIL is acknowledged. This means that curricula typically mention the global role of English as econocultural fact and give basically one or both of the following kinds of motivation for learning it: the utilitarian one, i.e. importance for international business, and the idealistic one, i.e. the potential it affords for furthering cross-cultural communication and mutual understanding.

On the meta-level of the global functions of English seem to have moved into a new phase recently: the late 1980's and early 1990's might be described as the era of linguistic imperialism views, focused on reckoning with the past. Now, in the early 2000's, it appears that we have entered an era in which a kind of functional realism and pragmatism view seems to establish itself.

In curricula, textbooks and reference materials, the focus is still largely on Anglo-American culture(s), plus sometimes 'exotic optional extras' such as post-colonial literature and New Englishes, but again through a predominantly British 'lens'. Standard British English or American English norms are taken for granted, the advocacy of 'authentic' materials constitutes a kind of pedagogical mantra, and teachers are expected to help their learners cope with 'real English', which is taken to be the English used by native speakers in their speech communities in e.g. the UK or the US. This 'real English' can, of course, now be described with unprecedented accuracy due to the availability of huge corpora of native English and the required technology for analysing these corpora. This has yielded a substantial crop of corpus-based teaching materials and reference works.

For the teaching of mother tongue English and, even more so, the (largely monolingual) teaching of English as a foreign language in the traditional sense this innovation/revolution in descriptive linguistics constitutes a potentially enormously important and welcome resource. However, these descriptions have also been adopted in completely different contexts, where the teaching should predominantly prepare for EIL rather than ENL use, without their relevance having been scrutinised and questioned.

6.3.1. Conceptual Considerations

Traditionally, the notion of a language is so closely and automatically tied up with its native speakers that it is very difficult to open up 'conceptual space' for EIL.

Coulmas points out,

> It is interesting to note that the nativeness criterion is maintained across theoretical boundaries and contrasts ... Within the framework of field linguistics, the native speaker is a human being who is able to give information about his or her language. In theoretical linguistics, by contrast, he often figures as an abstract idealisation. Yet, notwithstanding these fundamental differences, the speaker whom the linguist is concerned about is invariably claimed to be a *native* speaker. He is the one who can legitimately supply data, and his language is what grammatical analyses

> are meant to account for. Thus, nativeness is *the* only universally accepted criterion for authenticity.

More than 20 years after Coulmas made these observations, the general thrust of his argument still holds, but at least two additions are called for: from today's point of view, next to "field linguistics" in the quotation above there should also be "corpus linguistics". And 'nativised' varieties should be included in the considerations. These varieties, e.g. Indian English, Nigerian English, are interesting because the terms generally employed to refer to them reflect the problematic and crucial role of the nativeness criterion. At any rate, what this nomenclature shows is how deeply ingrained the notion of nativeness is in any considerations of language theorising, description and teaching, and hence how urgent, and how difficult, it is to shed the conceptual straightjacket of English as a native language when tackling the task of working out appropriate frameworks for EIL.

6.3.2. Linguistic Considerations

Even when functional and conceptual consensus about EIL will have been reached, this cannot have an impact on the teaching of EIL as long as no comprehensive and reliable description of salient features of EIL is available. This may sound controversial and utopian, but in fact empirical work on various levels of language has been under way for several years now. A number of descriptions and analyses of selected aspects of EIL use have been, and are being, conducted, in particular in the area of the (intercultural) pragmatics of 'non-native – non-native' communication in English. Nevertheless, some generalisations about the pragmatics of EIL can be made: misunderstandings are not frequent; when they do occur, they tend to be resolved either by topic change or, less often, by overt negotiation using communication strategies such as rephrasing and repetition. As long as a certain threshold of understanding is obtained, interlocutors seem to adopt what Firth has termed the 'let-it-pass principle', which gives the impression of EIL talk being overtly consensus-oriented, cooperative and mutually supportive, and thus appearing fairly robust. House sounds a more sceptical note, pointing to the danger that superficial consensus may well hide sources of trouble at a deeper level, a caveat that certainly needs to be taken seriously and investigated further. Other features of EIL pragmatics that House has pointed to are the tendency of interlocutors to behave in a fairly 'self-centred' way and to pursue their own agendas and to engage in series of 'parallel monologues' rather than dialogues.

While pragmatics is a fairly open-ended area and thus requires particularly large databases, phonology is a much more 'closed system'. It is therefore not surprising that the first book-length study of characteristics of EIL interaction should be available in this area, namely Jenkins' *The Phonology of English as an International Language*. Jenkins' work centres around "a pedagogical core of phonological intelligibility for speakers of EIL" which she was able to propose after establishing which pronunciation features impeded mutual intelligibility in her empirical studies of what she terms 'interlanguage talk' among 'non-native' speakers of English. This procedure provided an empirical basis for her suggestion "to scale down the phonological task for the majority of learners by ... focusing pedagogic attention on those items which are essential in terms of intelligible pronunciation" and to prioritise features which constitute more relevant and more realistic learning targets for EIL speakers. These features constitute Jenkins' *Lingua Franca Core*. Jenkins' Lingua Franca Core does not include, for instance, some sounds which are regarded, and taught, as 'particularly English' ones by most learners and teachers, such as the '*th*-sounds' and the 'dark l' allophone. In the conversations analysed by Jenkins, mastery of these sounds proved not to be crucial for mutual intelligibility and so various substitutions, such as /f, v/ or /s, z/ or /t, d/ for the '*th*-sounds' are permissible, and indeed also found in some native-speaker varieties. The '*th*-sounds' and the 'dark l' are therefore designated 'non-core'.

The same is true of the following features:

- Vowel quality
- Weak forms
- Other features of connected speech such as assimilation
- Pitch direction to signal attitude or grammatical meaning
- Word stress placement
- Stress-timing

On the other hand, there were features which proved decisive for EIL intelligibility and which therefore constitute the phonological Lingua Franca Core:

- The consonant inventory with the exception of the '*th*-sounds' and of 'dark l'.
- Additional phonetic requirements: aspiration of word-initial /p/, /t/, and /k/, which were otherwise frequently heard as their lenis counterparts /b/, /d/, and /g/ and the maintenance of length before lenis consonants, e.g. the longer /æ/ in the word *sad* contrasted with the phonetically shorter one in the word *sat*.
- Consonant clusters: no omission of sounds in word-initial clusters, e.g. in *proper* and *strap*.
- Vowel sounds: maintenance of the contrast between long and short vowels, such as the long and short *i*-sounds in the words *leave* and*live.*
- Production and placement of nuclear (tonic) stress, especially when used contrastively. (e.g. *He came by TRAIN* vs. *He CAME by train*).

6.3.3. Pedagogic Considerations

The desirability of at least considering EIL as a realistic learning goal has been broached from various angles in publications for well quite some time now. However, these fairly scarce exhortations to rethink the teaching of English have not had any significant impact on mainstream curriculum planning over the last two decades or so. It would be interesting to speculate why this is the case. One factor to be taken into account in this respect is certainly the enormous influence of research in ENL countries that has been, partly rather uncritically, assumed to be of a priori relevance to teaching in Europe, notably work on second language acquisition and corpus linguistics in the US and the UK, which generally take the primacy of standard native speaker norms as self-evident. This could be regarded, to use Widdowson's terms, as a case of 'linguistics applied' taking precedence over developments in applied linguistics which otherwise might have evolved continuously from the early 1980's.

However, a more obvious obstacle to the adoption of EIL for teaching has been the absence of sufficient descriptive work on EIL, which would be a necessary requirement as a component of EIL-focused curricula. With the linguistic research now being carried out with increasing intensity, this lack is gradually being remedied. In addition, both the perceived rate of globalisation in general, and the spread of English as the epiphenomenona accompanying it, have speeded up in recent years, particularly due to the pervasive influence of the Internet. Lastly, the spate of literature on indigenised varieties of English in post-colonial contexts coupled with that on linguistic imperialism and critical discourse analysis are likely to have contributed to a more widespread awareness of and resistance to traditional assumptions.

References

Ammon, U., "Towards more fairness in international English: Linguistic rights of non-native speakers?", In: Phillipson, R. (ed.) *Rights to Language: Equity, Power, and Education, Celebrating the 60th Birthday of Tove Skutnabb-Kangas*. Mahwah, New Jersey: Lawrence Erlbaum Associates, 2000.

Bamgbose, A., "Torn between the norms: innovations in world Englishes", *World Englishes,* 1998.

Bhatia, V.K., *Analysing Genre: Language Use in Professional Settings,* London: Longman, 1993.

Biber, D., Johansson, S., Leech, G., Conrad, S. & Finegan, E., *Longman Grammar of Spoken and Written English,* Harlow, Essex: Pearson, 1999.

Brumfit, C.J. (ed.), *English for International Communication,* Oxford: Pergamon, 1982.

Brumfit, C.J., *Individual Freedom in Language Teaching: Helping Learners to Develop a Dialect of their Own,* Oxford: Oxford University Press, 2001.

Brutt-Griffler, J., *World English,* Clevedon: Multilingual Matters, 2002.

Buttjes, D. & Byram, M. (eds.), *Mediating Languages and Cultures: Towards an Intercultural Theory of Foreign Language Education,* Clevedon: Multilingual Matters, 1990.

Byram, M. and Fleming, M. (eds.), *Language Learning in Intercultural Perspective,* Cambridge: Cambridge University Press, 1998.

Byram, M. & Zarate, G. (eds.), *The Sociocultural and Intercultural Dimension of Language Learning and Teaching,* Strasbourg: Council of Europe, 1997.

Canagarajah, S., *Resisting Linguistic Imperialism in English Teaching,* Oxford: Oxford University Press, 1999.

Crystal, D., *English as a Global Language,* Cambridge: Cambridge University Press, 1997.

Granger, S. (ed.), *Learner English on Computer,* London: Longman, 1998.

Greenbaum, S. (ed.), *Comparing English Worldwide, The International Corpus of English,* Oxford: Clarendon, 1996.

James, C. & Garrett, P. (eds.), *Language Awareness in the Classroom,* London: Longman, 1991.

Jenkins, J., "Which pronunciation norms and models for English as an International Language?" *ELT Journal,* 1998.

________________., *The Phonology of English as an International Language,* Oxford: Oxford University Press, 2000.

McKay, S., *Teaching English as an International Language,* Oxford: Oxford University Press, 2002.

Pennycook, A., *The Cultural Politics of English as an International Language,* London: Longman,1994.

Smith, L.E. (ed.), *Readings in English as an International Language,* Oxford: Pergamon,1983.

Widdowson, H.G., "EIL, ESL, EFL: global issues and local interests", *World Englishes,*1997.

7

Development of World Englishes

The terms 'New Englishes' or 'World Englishes' become customary to use the plural form 'Englishes' to stress the diversity to be found in the language today, and to stress that English no longer has one single base of authority, prestige and normativity. The term 'World English' runs the risk of being over-general, since British English is not generally studied within this paradigm. Yet one might quibble that it is a 'World English' too. The term is often cited as parallel to the term 'World Music', which covers 'non-Western' musical forms. In all of these terms there is a problem of perspective that is difficult to overcome.

The following are the different perspective of World Englishes:

(a) *Pidgin Englishes*: Pidgins are defined prototypically as rudimentary languages that have no native speakers, though they may subsequently gain in complexity. They arise from trade and other—largely colonial—forms of contact. English-based pidgins like West African pidgin English may be considered to belong to the English family, since they are 'lexified' by English—i.e. English is the source of much of their vocabulary.

(b) *Creole Englishes*: Creoles are fully developed speech forms, which show so much restructuring as to bear little resemblance grammatically to their luxuries. These languages are 'mixed' in the sense that typically their grammars and lexicons come from different sources

(c) *English as a Second Language (ESL):* Typically these are varieties that arose in countries where English was introduced in the colonial era in either face-to-face communication or (more usually) via the education system of a country in which there is, or had once been, a sizeable number of speakers of English. In ESL countries like Kenya, Sri Lanka and Nigeria, English plays a key role in education, government and education.

(d) *English as a Foreign Language (EFL)*: This category typically refers to the English used in countries in which its influence has been external, rather than via a body of 'settlers'. For EFL speakers English plays a role for mainly *international* rather than *intra*national purposes. Whereas ESL countries produce literature in English (and other languages), EFL countries typically do not use English in creative writing. The trend towards globalisation in economics, communication and culture has made EFL prominent in places like China, Europe, Brazil, etc

(e) *Immigrant Englishes*: In the context of migration to an Englishdominant country, varieties of English which originate as EFLs may retain some distinctiveness or may merge with the regional English of their territory, depending on a host of social and economic factors. Thus whilst English in Mexico is of the EFL variety, Chicano English of the USA shows greater affinity with general US English. However, Chicano English is still a distinct variety amongst many speakers which we classify as an 'immigrant English'.

(f) *Language-shift Englishes*: These are varieties that develop when English replaces the erstwhile primary language(s) of a community. There is, nevertheless, frequently a sense of continuity with the ancestral language(s) and culture(s) in the shifting community. The difference between 'language-shift English' and 'social dialect' is one of degree; the former can, in time, shade into a social dialect.

(g) *Jargon Englishes*: Whereas a pidgin is a well-defined (if rudimentary) variety, with norms that are tacitly agreed upon by its speakers, a jargon is characterised by great individual variation and instability (hence also described as a pre-pidgin). E.g. contact between South Sea Islanders and Europeans in the nineteenth century led to the formation of unstable jargons in many parts of the Pacific.

One of these developed into a stable, expanded pidgin, Tok Pisin, which is now one of the official languages of Papua New Guinea.

(h) *Hybrid Englishes*: Also called 'bilingual mixed languages', these are versions of English which occur in code-mixing in many urban centres where a local language comes into contact with English. Although sometimes given derogatory names, like Hinglish for the hybrid Hindi-English of north Indian cities, these hybrids may have prestige amongst urban youth and the young at heart in informal styles.

In the first place our characterisation suffers from focusing on 'products' rather than 'processes'. Sociolinguists generally try to avoid the bias of conceiving of language in terms of already codified forms (as in grammars and dictionaries) or written norms. They argue that language is constantly being made and remade by speakers in terms of their situation, need, interlocutor, audience, knowledge of other 'languages', general strategies of communication, etc.

Secondly, we advocate a 'prototype' definition of the term 'English', with some varieties considered clear-cut examples. We also accept that the boundaries of terms are fuzzy, so that some Englishes may have overlapping memberships. The following are examples of phenomena with multiple memberships:

(a) English hybrids—e.g. the mixed variety of English and Malay, described by Baskaran;

(b) decreolising English Creoles—e.g. the continuum between Creole and Caribbean English in Jamaica, described by de Camp;

(c) underworld slang—e.g. the grafting of an 'antilanguage' lexicon onto English grammar in Elizabethan cant, as described by Halliday.

An institutionalised English is one that has been introduced formally in a territory via education and is used in some civil, administrative and governmental functions. A performance variety is one which does not have this backing and is reliant on ad hoc skills of communication that individuals may pick up via EFL education or via brief contacts with tourists, traders, etc.

Performance varieties include EFLs, jargons, rudimentary pidgins and so forth. Another indication of overlapping memberships concerns the intermediate status of 'Protectorates' in the former British empire—territories that were not fully colonised but which did receive educational and other infrastructural support from Britain to wrest them away from the influence of rival imperialists. Territories such as Egypt and the southern African kingdom of Lesotho may well have a status intermediate between ESL and EFL territories. The spread of English in Europe in more recent times calls into question whether territories like Holland and Scandinavia are still EFL or whether they are moving towards ESL.

Notions like 'immigrant English' are also dependent on sociohistorical factors. This is not a term that is commonly used in the literature, where writers simply use the general label ESL. Target language (TL) makes it possible to avoid the specifics of whether the target is standard English or a regional or social dialect, or whether British, American or other norms are involved. Another useful term for more or less the same concept is 'superstrate' language, which stresses issues of power and accessibility. Whilst 'TL' implies a second-language-acquisition perspective in which the target is more or less available (inside or outside of classrooms), 'superstrate' leaves it open whether the dominant colonial language is accessible to new learners or not. In Pidgin and Creole studies 'superstrate' contrasts with 'substrate(s)', the original language(s) of the group of speakers who are in a subordinate position in terms of power and status. In the study of pidgins and Creoles it is argued that though English often was a source of vocabular, it was not really the target of acquisition, since on many plantations slaves were interested in developing a medium of inter-ethnic communication, rather than mastering the colonial language.

The balance between English and the mother tongue in the immigrant English context is not as clearly defined as in an ESL territory. Special conditions like the intention to return to the homeland or a heightened sense of ethnicity may run counter to this tendency. ESL is essentially an abbreviation for the acquisition of English under conditions of additive bilingualism, i.e. the addition of a socially relevant language to a community's repertoire. Immigrant Englishes (and language-shift Englishes) are frequently implicated in subtractive bilingualism, that is unstable bilingualism resulting in the gradual loss of a community's erstwhile language. Finally—regarding question—there are indeed overlaps between a language-shift English and a social dialect. The former term (language-shift English) is desirable and necessary if one is interested in the process of shift and acquisition, rather than the ultimate 'social dialect' product.

7.1. WES, ELF and World Standard English

As Bolton points out, there are three possible interpretations of the expression *World Englishes.* Firstly, it serves as an "umbrella label" covering all varieties of English worldwide and the different approaches used to describe and analyse them. Secondly, it is used in a narrower sense to refer to the so-called new Englishes in Africa, Asia, and the Caribbean. Thirdly, it is used to represent the pluricentric approach to the study of English associated with Kachru and his colleagues, and often referred to as the *Kachruvian* approach, although there is considerable overlap between this and the second interpretation of the term. The first use is also sometimes represented by other terms, including World English (i.e., in the singular), international English(es), and *global English(es),* while the second is in fact more commonly represented by the terms nativised, indigenised, institutionalised, and new Englishes or *English as a second language.* And still other terms are currently in circulation. Despite the range of interpretations of the term *World Englishes* and its alternatives, however, the links between them are so strong, and the field now so well established, that there seems to be little confusion over the intended reference.

The same cannot be said, by contrast, for ELF, despite Larry Smith's visionary work on English as an international language dating way back to the 1970s and 1980s. One complication for ELF is the fact that *international English* is sometimes used as shorthand for English as an international language, or EIL, itself an alternative term for ELF. Used in this way, it can be misleading because, as Seidlhofer points out, "it suggests that there is one clearly distinguishable, codified, and unitary variety called International English, which is certainly not the case". Thus, in one sense, *international English* is used to refer to the local

Englishes of those non–mother tongue countries where it has an intranational institutionalised role, although some researchers also include the mother tongue English countries in their definitions. On the other hand, *international English* is also used in another sense to refer to the use of English as a means of international communication across national and linguistic boundaries.

Unfortunately, some WEs scholars assume that ELF (EIL) refers to the same phenomenon as WS(S)E and then criticise ELF (EIL) for promoting a monocentric view of English based on American or British norms rather than a pluricentric view based on local norms. However, nothing could be further from the truth. Firstly, far from prioritising inner circle norms, ELF researchers specifically exclude mother tongue speakers from their data collection. Indeed, in its purest form, ELF is defined as a contact language used only among non–mother tongue speakers. For example, according to House, "ELF interactions are defined as interactions between members of two or more different linguacultures in English, *for none of whom English is the mother tongue* ". The majority of ELF researchers nevertheless accept that speakers of English from both inner and outer circles also participate in intercultural communication (albeit as a small minority in the case of inner circle speakers), so do not define ELF communication this narrowly. In their search to discover the ways in which ELF interactions are sui generis, as House puts it, they nevertheless restrict data collection to interactions among non–mother tongue speakers. And if the point is reached when ELF forms can be codified, they believe that as far as ELF interactions are concerned, any participating mother tongue speakers will have to follow the agenda set by ELF speakers, rather than vice versa, as has been the case up to now.

Although ELF researchers seek to identify frequently and systematically used forms that differ from inner circle forms without causing communication problems and override first language groupings, their purpose is not to describe and codify a single ELF variety. The existence of ELF is not intended to imply that learners should aim for an English that is identical in all respects. ELF researchers do not believe any such monolithic variety of English does or ever will exist. Rather, they believe that anyone participating in international communication needs to be familiar with, and have in their linguistic repertoire for use, as and when appropriate, certain forms (phonological, lexicogrammatical, etc.) that are widely used and widely intelligible across groups of English speakers from different first language backgrounds. This is why accommodation is so highly valued in ELF research. At the same time, ELF does not at all discourage speakers from learning and using their local variety in local communicative contexts, regardless of whether this is an inner, outer, or expanding circle English.

The tensions nevertheless remain, and some scholars of outer circle Englishes continue to contest the legitimacy of ELF, much as the legitimacy of outer circle Englishes was contested in the past. Such scholars continue to describe the expanding circle Englishes indiscriminately as EFL varieties, in other words, English learned as a foreign language for use in communication with native speakers. For example, Bolton, in his survey of the world's Englishes, outlines Kachru's three circle model, which characterises expanding circle varieties as "norm-dependent", without further comment and does not mention ELF (or EIL) at all. Thus, he ignores the fact that the three circle model "is not designed to deal with the characteristic functioning of the language in the Expanding Circle, as a lingua franca". One frequent and misplaced criticism of ELF made by WEs scholars is that it supposedly ignores the pluricentric nature of English. For example, in the call for papers for their edited collection, the editors claimed that an alternative viewpoint to EIL is one which acknowledges the polymorphous nature of the English language worldwide, identifying different varieties under a World Englishes paradigm, [whose emphasis] is not on prescribing either a reduced or extended form of standard English, but on questioning the very concept of "standard," and on advocating a pluricentric model rather than a monolithic one.

Kachru in fact argues against the entire notion of ELF on the basis that the term is not being used in its original sense, and that it is "loaded", although he does not explain how. Despite the controversy surrounding ELF research, the phenomenon seems slowly to be gaining recognition in East Asia, Europe, and to a lesser extent, Latin America. It is also beginning to gain the approval of sociolinguists in the way that the outer circle Englishes have already done. Whether in another 15 years, it will have made progress comparable to that made by the indigenised Englishes over the past 15, and whether either ELF or WEs will have made greater inroads into TESOL practice, remains to be seen.

7.2. Developments in WES and ELF Research

Y. Kachru neatly categorises WEs research interests as follows: the historical background to the spread of English; the linguistic processes responsible for features among varieties; the sociocultural contexts of English use; intelligibility both across varieties and within indigenised varieties in their local settings, together with the role of code-mixing and codeswitching; the impact of English on local languages, or *Englishisation* and, conversely, the impact of local languages on English, or *nativisation;* bilingualism and multilingualism; literary creativity in institutionalised settings; the functional allocation of varieties within English-using communities; the communicative needs of users which underlie observed linguistic differences; and, the teaching and learning of English in the outer and expanding circles.

Starting with corpus-based research, most corpora to be collected have tended to focus on British and American Englishes. However, this 15-year period is noteworthy for the small but growing availability of corpora that include outer circle Englishes, with expanding circle corpora in the pipeline. This period has also seen an increase in dictionaries and grammars of different Englishes such as *The Macquarie Dictionary*, which includes words from a range of Southeast Asian Englishes. European Englishes have lagged some way behind their Asian counterparts in terms of research. This lag has been caused at least in part, it seems, by an assumption that European Englishes are not legitimate varieties because they did not arise through colonisation and have not undergone a process of institutionalisation.

Speakers of European Englishes are typically also speakers of ELF, to the extent that they learn and use English more for interlinguacultural communication than to communicate with speakers who share the their first linguaculture . The same is true of many English speakers in other regions of the world, such as parts of East Asia and throughout Latin America. Despite the fact that those who use English primarily as a lingua franca are thought to constitute the world's largest group of English speakers, research into ELF only began around 1990.

This rapid spread of English has evoked different reactions among linguists and sociolinguists, as well as politicians and governments. Since the seventies, a number of liberal sociolinguists have called for the demolition of linguistic hegemony. Phillipson, for example, coined the term "linguistic imperialism" to describe the spread of English as being analogous to economic and military imperialism. He saw the linguistic domination of English as not only economical but also cultural and ideological, and suggested ways of countering it by language planning policies. Others, however, took a more pragmatic view and saw the global spread of English as natural, neutral and beneficial. For example, Kachru maintained that the spread of English was a positive development in the twentieth century world context, regardless of the reasons for its earlier spread. For Kachru, the debate is whether a central standard should be maintained or whether different varieties of English should be legitimised. For many years, Kachru has been advocating the institutionalisation of non-native varieties of English, hence the term World Englishes.

According to Kachru, the term "Englishes" "symbolises the functional and formal variations, divergent sociolinguistic contexts, ranges and varieties of English in creativity, and various types of acculturation in parts of the Western and non-Western world. This concept emphasises 'WE-ness', and not the dichotomy between us and them (the native and the non-native users)." Kachru goes as far as to suggest that English is an Asian language. The viability of World Englishes for international communication has been questioned, however. If a country's long-term interest in English is econocultural, then the model of English that is needed is one which will not impede international communication. It is only when a country's interest in English is merely for intranational communication that a local variety of English is feasible.

References

Adamson, B., *China's English: A history of English in Chinese education*, Hong Kong SAR, China: University of Hong Kong Press, 2004.

Ammon, U., "Towards more fairness in international English: Linguistic rights of non-native speakers", In R. Phillipson (Ed.), *Rights to language. Equity, power, and education,* Mahwah, N.J.: Lawrence Erlbaum, 2000.

Bailey, R. W., *Images of English: A cultural history of the language,* Ann Arbor: University of Michigan Press, 1991.

Berns, M., & Friedrich, P. (Eds.), "Special issue on English in South America: A different kind of difference", [Special issue], *World Englishes,* 2003.

Block, D., *The social turn in second language acquisition,* Edinburgh, Scotland: University of Edinburgh Press, 2003.

Bolton, K., *Chinese Englishes,* Cambridge, England: Cambridge University Press, 2003.

_______________., "World Englishes", In A. Davies & C. Elder (Eds.), *The handbook of applied linguistics* (pp. 369–396). Oxford, England: Blackwell, 2004.

Cheshire, J. (Ed.), *English around the world,* Cambridge, England: Cambridge University Press, 1991.

Modiano, M., "International English in the global village", *English Today,* 1999a.

Pennycook, A., *The cultural politics of English as an international language,* London: Longman, 1994.

Quirk, R., "Language varieties and standard language", *English Today,* 1990.

8

English: The Language of Internet

The importance of the Internet grows rapidly in all fields of human life, including not only research and education but also marketing and trade as well as entertainment and hobbies. This implies that it becomes more and more important to know how to use Internet services and, as a part of this, to read and write English. Of course, the majority of mankind cannot use the Internet nowadays or in the near future, since they live in countries which lack the necessary economical and technological infrastructure. But the Internet causes polarisation in developed countries, too: people are divided into Internet users and Internet illiterates, and as the use of the Internet grows and often replaces traditional methods of communication, the illiterates may find themselves in an awkward position.

In general, it is easy to learn to use Internet services. The worst problems of Internet illiteracy are, in addition to lack of economical resources of course, wrong attitudes. Older people are usually not accustomed to live in a world of continuous and rapid change, and they may not realise the importance of the Internet or the easiness of learning to use it. But although Internet services themselves are, generally speaking, easy to learn and use, you will find yourself isolated on the Internet if you are not familiar with English. This means that knowledge or lack of knowledge of English is one of the most severe factors that cause polarisation.

Learning to use a new Internet service or user interface may take a few hours, a few days, or even weeks, but it takes years to learn a language so that you can use it in a fluent and self-confident manner. Of course, when you know some English, you can learn more just by using it on the Internet, but at least currently the general tendency among Internet users is to discourage people in their problems with the English language. Incorrect English causes a few flames much more probably than encouragement and friendly advice.

In different countries and cultures, English has different positions. There are countries where English is the native language of the majority, there are countries where English is a widely known second language, and there are countries where English has no special position. These differences add to the above-mentioned polarisation. Specifically, it is difficult for people in previous colonies of other countries than Great Britain (e.g. France, Spain, the Netherlands) to adapt to the necessity of learning English. Locally, it may be necessary to learn the language of the previous colonial power since it is often an official language and the common language of educated people; globally, English is necessary for living on the Internet. And the more languages you have to learn well, the less time and energy you will have for learning other things.

Things can change, and they actually do, often with unpredictable speed. The rapid fall of the Soviet empire—including the loss of the role of Russian as a "universal" language within in—is a recent indication of this. English can lose its position as a widely used (although not official) universal language in two ways. Either a new empire emerges and its language becomes universal, or a constructed language becomes very popular.

8.1. English as a Universal Language

Apart from being widely used and known, English is extremely unsuitable as a universal language. There are several reasons to this. Any national language, i.e. a language which is or was originally the language of a particular tribe or nation, has obvious defects when used for international communication:

- Native speakers of the language are in a quite different position than others. Some people regard this as bad in itself, as contrary to the equality principle. Native speakers tend to use idioms and rare words and to speak too fast, unless they exercise conscious control over their language—and such control is difficult and unnatural when applied to one's mother tongue.

- National languages exist in various dialects and forms—sometimes they are even mutually unintelligible, but the differences always make communication harder. There is usually no standard for a national language, and even if something that can be called standard exists, it is just one form of the language—typically a form that is only used by a minority, and even by it only in a minority of occasions. For a native speaker of a language, it is natural to use one's own dialect, and it is difficult to avoid this entirely; this emphasizes the importance of the above-mentioned problem of native speakers expressing themselves in international contexts.
- When you learn your native language in your childhood, you learn it by listening to and talking with people who have it as their native language. First they know it much better than you, later equally well. Thus it is very natural human behaviour to use your native language with the unconscious but strong assumption that the listener or reader knows the language to the same or even higher extent than you. In international contexts, this built-in assumption is almost always false, and this has severe consequences.
- A national language carries with it the history of the nation. For instance, words and phrases have got, in addition to their dictionary meanings, connotations, colours and associations. This is an important cultural phenomenon which helps in keeping the nation a nation, but in international communication it is a burden.
- National languages have originally evolved as spoken languages. When written national languages originated, they were usually formed on the basis of the dialect of the capital or other important area, with the aim of creating a language which supports the creation of a unified nation. Thus, the very origin of a national language is in a sense nationalistic, not internationalistic.
- Due to their long history, national languages have historical relics and features which make them illogical and irrational, such as grammatical gender or irregular forms. Moreover, being originally spoken languages, they lack

> sufficient tools for expressing things in an exact, unambiguous manner; and the need for such expression is immense and growing, especially in the areas of law and contracts, technology and technical descriptions, and science.

These remarks apply to English, too, and especially to English. One of the worst relics of English is the orthography. English has a very rich repertoire of idioms, and it typically has several words which have the same basic meaning but different connotations and stylistic value. Especially in international contexts you can never know what words mean to people with different backgrounds. Thus, you may occasionally get your basic message understood in some way, but you cannot tell in which way. This is of course an inherent problem in all human communication, but the nature of English makes it a really big problem.

English is an eclectic language which tends to borrow words from other languages instead of constructing words for new concepts from older words with derivation or word composition. People often say that English has a rich vocabulary as if it were something to be proud of. The richness of the vocabulary results basically from word borrowing and implies that words for related concepts are typically not related to each other in any obvious, regular manner. Word borrowing makes a language more international in one sense, but in the essential sense it makes it less suitable for international communication, since learning the vocabulary is more difficult.

8.1.1. Constructed Language for International Communication

It is well known that a large number of attempts to that effect have been made, with little results. Advocates of the basic idea have hardly agreed on anything but the basic idea, and most constructed languages have had no use as a language. People who strongly support the idea have typically designed their own proposal, a perfect language, and they do not want accept anything that is not perfect—"best" is the worst enemy of "good".

The very idea is not inherently unrealistic, but it can only be realised if strong economical and political interests are involved, such as the intended creation of a European or Japanese-Chinese empire. The best that the advocates of a constructed international language can wish is that such empires emerge and that the United States remain as an important power, so that the world will have a few strong empires which cannot beat each other but must live in parallel and in cooperation. In such a situation, it might turn out that it is unrealistic not to agree on a common language which is not any of the national languages.

The role of the Internet in this hypothetical development would be to create the informational infrastructure for the discussion of the construction of the language, the very construction work, spreading out information about the language, the use of the language, and continuous development of the language. Most probably the language would first be used in parallel with English, and the initial use would be for such purposes like international agreements where national languages are clearly insufficient. For instance, if you need to formulate an agreement between two countries, you definitely need a neutral common language instead of having the text in two languages, each text allowing its own interpretations.

8.1.2. Machine Translation

During the last few decades, quite a lot of predictions and even promises have been presented regarding machine translation, but useful software and systems for it have not been available until recently. This has caused disappointments and pessimism to the extent that many people consider machine translation as definitely unrealistic. Actually, machine translation is operational for a wide range of texts, although corrective actions by human translators may be necessary. Corrections are needed to resolve ambiguities which exist due to the limitations of the software and to fix errors caused by the fact that translation of human languages requires extralinguistic information.

Assumably fully automatic correct translation will never be possible. However, this does not exclude the possibility of using it extensively. It only means that we must be prepared to accept a risk—decreasing by advances in technology, but never reaching zero—of translation errors. Such risks exist when human translators are used, too, and in many respects automatic translation can be more reliable. Both human beings and computer programs err, in different ways.

In addition to the advancement of translation techniques, there are several ways in which the risk of errors in automatic translation can be decreased:

- *avoiding ambiguities in the source language:* people can try to write their texts so that they are more easily tractable by translation programs
- *checking the translations:* a person who has written a text in his native language may run it through a translation program, check and correct the result, and provide the "authorised" translation together with the source text; although it is usually not feasible to do this for several target languages, the authorised translation (typically, to English) can be used by translation programs for checking purposes: if translations from the original source and the authorised translation yield different results, this fact should be signalled to the user
- *warnings:* in general, problematic fragments of texts like those obviously allowing different syntactic analyses, can be signalled to the user—i.e. to the author, to the reader, or both.

Currently the operational machine translation software is essentially based on syntactic analysis, so that semantic information is implicit in the dictionaries used by the software. An alternative approach, based on some kind of semantic analysis in addition to syntax, does not appear to be practically applicable yet.

8.2. Dominance of English in the Internet

The dominance of English in the Internet needs no arguing for. Computers are in any case English-oriented. Netscape and Java are in English, the vocabulary of computing and of the Internet is overwhelmingly English, and most of the texts that are accessed through it are in English. The search engines are in English and are in the US. The reasons for the dominance of English are firstly historical—the Internet began in the USA, which is still the leading user of it, and the USA is an English-using nation. The norms of the Internet are established in ASCII texts, and even now texts transmitted unaltered from (for example) Francophone keyboards may produce garbage on English-favouring keyboards.

Two things constrain the use of languages other than English on world-wide web documents and communications:

- the difficulty of writing languages using non-ASCII characters, and characters that have diacritics
- the desire to reach as large a readership as possible.

The first of these constraints can be overcome (as in the case of Tamil), though not necessarily with ease. The second constraint, however, means that most documents in languages other than English, including those in countries where English is little used internally are mirrored by English translations. The world wide web is in the position of a permanent international conference, where papers are either in English or are accompanied by English translations. The role of English reflects the dominance of English in cross-national communication.

8.2.1. Access to the Internet

Access to the Internet is empowering. It gives access to uncensored material of enormous variety. Access to a world-size (though rather messy) encyclopedia. Access to almost instant communication with individuals located thousands of miles away. A person using the Internet can adopt a new persona—you can change gender, acquire beauty, lose disability, develop aggression....... There is information available, entertainment, insight into other cultures. Various governments (including those of the USA, France, and Singapore) have attempted to control some of this information, either in terms of what can be placed in URLs or in terms of what can downloaded. But so far no effective way of controlling the reading of documents placed on the web has been found.

However, this empowerment has on the whole been extended most to those who are already most empowered. To gain good access to the web three things are needed:

- to live in a location that supports the technology needed to gain access
- to have access to a service provider
- to be able to use English

In many countries which do have Internet access, large portions of the population live in rural areas away from the electricity and telephone provision that supports this basic access, or are not wealthy enough to have such facilities themselves. Even within wealthy countries with effective electricity and telephone systems, the nearest service provider may be sufficiently far from some rural users to make accessing the web prohibitively expensive, due to the cost of long distance or satellite telephone calls.

After the establishment of the Internet by the military in the USA, it was universities that first took advantage of the web. To this day, academic users of the web (mostly on edu and ac servers) are especially privileged. They have unusually free access to the Internet, seldom paying for their own access time, and seldom accountable for their use of it. In some universities there may be corporate constraints on the Internet-users' freedom to develop their own sites. Users in commercial organisations and governmental organisations generally experience less freedom.

In many countries access through educational, commercial and governmental bodies preceded the availability of private Internet accounts, and corporate users still dominate the Internet. France is in the unusual position of having been a pioneer in giving private access to computer link systems, through the hugely popular Minitel system, developed long before the Internet became available on the scale it has been in the 1990s. The success of Minitel (with over 7 million access points in France) is one of the factors that has made access to the Internet in France rather low, as so many people had become accustomed to using the cheap and familiar Minitel. This has presented an economic, technological, and cultural obstacle to the widespread use of the Internet in France. Minitel is still the dominant text based communication system in France, although it is now linked to the Internet.

Private access to the Internet has developed over the 1990s, although there are still technical and commercial problems in private accounts, as the recent blocakages at America Online have shown. Many countries have been slow to provide private access to the Internet. Even where private access is possible, it is costly, with rental fees and telephone costs being added to very substantial hardware costs. In the UK, for example, the average cost of a computer is around £2000. The average weekly earnings of full-time employees on adult rates is £336.30. Thus someone in full time work would have to spend 6 weeks' salary on a computer. The lower the national and individual salary, the more this cost becomes out of reach. In countries with lower average salaries, computers tend to be more expensive both in real and proportional terms.

The first two things needed for Internet access make it an advantage:

- to be in a country with good electricity supply, good telephonic connections and the political will to allow Internet access
- within those countries, to be an academic user, a user with other corporate access, or wealthy enough to afford a private account

These requirements, essentially economic in foundation, point to countries with high GNP, and to an urban environment within them.

8.2.2. Distribution of English Users

However, the third thing helpful for Internet access, the ability to use English, divides the world into rather different groupings. Sociolinguists (e.g. Moag) have traditionally grouped countries into three categories according to the dominant pattern of English use within them:

- *English as a native language*: Most people grow up speaking English at home. English the dominant language of daily usage for most people. (examples: UK, USA, Australia)
- *English as a second language*: Those who know English mostly learnt it after they had learned another language. English often learnt at school. English is used (by varying proportions of the population) in everyday and in official usage, with citizens often speaking to each other in English. (examples: India, Singapore, Ghana, Philippines)
- *English as a foreign language*: Those who know English mostly learnt it at school. English is hardly ever spoken

within the country (outside English lessons). (Examples: France, Japan, Thailand)

EN/ESL countries are however poorly represented in Europe, where only the UK and Ireland (both ENL) historically represent this kind of intimate involvement with English. In Europe, only the Northwestern countries (especially Norway, Sweden, Finland, Denmark and the Netherlands) have achieved an extent of English use comparable to that in most former colonies. The difference in knowledge of English between ESL South Asia and ENL Southern Europe was illustrated in December 1996 when a boat full of would-be immigrants to Europe from South Asia sank off the coast of Greece.

Within the ESL countries a high level of use of English is virtually universal among precisely those socio-economic groups who have access to the Internet. In these countries, being educated and knowing English go hand in hand. Within most of the ENL countries, however, a privileged, highly educated position is no guarantee of access to English. Thus, in practice, the usefulness of English in the Internet places someone from a poor ESL country who has access to the Internet at a considerable advantage over someone from a much richer ENL country who does not know English or does not know it well.

8.2.3. Socio-political Implications

The Internet was established by, and still is dominated by, that most rich and central nation, the USA. Much Internet communication is routed through US servers, as all of us outside the US are only too aware. The centre of the Internet is the US. However, access to the Internet does weaken the geographical sense of centre in a number of ways. Although accessing a site overseas may be slower than accessing a local site, there are times of day in all locations when overseas sites are as fast to access as local ones, thus equalising the cost of access all over the world. E-mail, unlike telephone, fax, and postal mail, gives equally fast and cheap access to correspondents anywhere.

In all countries, however wealthy, access to the Internet is unevenly distributed, and in those countries which are anglophone postcolonial, the widespread knowledge of English among those who have Internet access places them at an advantage over equivalent people in ENL countries.

The culture of the Internet is still a predominantly American one. Users of the Internet become acculturated to its norms and to a style of presentation of self and of discourse which is essentially still American. At the same time, as more Internet users from outside the US participate in the Internet, the culture of the Internet will in part internationalised. A major factor in determining the extent to which acculturation or internationalisation prevails will be the participation of users in ESL anglophone postcolonial settings. If more people in the Anglophone countries of Africa could participate, this would be a major contribution to a balanced internationalisation.

The participation of the non-Anglophone countries of Europe in the internationalisation of the Internet is at present limited in part by lack of knowledge of or confidence in English. The Internet is one of a number of pressures on those countries resulting in increasing learning of English. However, in those countries (and even in the countries of North west Europe where English is more widely known) English is not indigenised—it is not seen as a local possession in the way that it is in the ENL and ESL countries, in both of which English can be part of an expression of a cultural identity. Thus, participants in the Internet from EFL countries have no vested interest in re-locating the dominant American-led culture of the Internet. The knowledge of English in the ESL countries allows them to be brokers, who, along with the non-American EFL countries, could re-culturate the Internet to a more genuinely international environment.

8.3. Dominance of the English Language in Communicating on the Internet

The Internet is a global, virtual community of worldwide success. It is a global success ensuring the almost simultaneous interaction between of billions of people not only from different backgrounds but also of different corners of the world. And the language used by the overwhelming majority connected to the Internet is English. The English language has come to dominate communication on the Internet, having met only a timid resistance so far, despite its obvious unsuitability as a lingua franca.

8.3.1. Linguistic Domination of English

One of the main reasons for this widespread dominance is that the centre of the Internet, still, is the United States and its culture is American. Moreover, it was invented in the United States from where it spread all around the world. As the US is the main user of the Internet and the US is and English-speaking nation, computers and software are still very much English oriented—although it is fair to say that programs have started to be adapted to various other languages. The most popular search engines are in English and are in the US. Also, let us not forget the very little mentioned English Commonwealth, the remnants of the British Empire where the English language is, if not the national language—as it is in Australia—then, an official second language—as is the case in India, for instance. However, since the Internet is so far-reaching and is such an excellent vehicle for knowledge, using English maximises the number of people who will understand you and your work.

English has no official status and the majority of observers and analysts agree that it never will. It is simply the contested language of power. The emergence of non-English sites is hampered by two main constraints: the ASCII code (American Standard Code for Information Interchange) that constitutes the basis for the standard, English keyboard, making it difficult for writing in non-ASCII characters and the already mentioned desire to reach a large a readership as possible. If the first constraint may be overcome despite the obvious intricacies, the second means that non-English documents and web-sites have to coexist with English counterparts and English translations.

8.3.2. Suitability of English

From the very beginning, we can say that the English language is extremely unsuitable as a universal language. There are various reasons for this affirmation. Firstly, it is a national language and it is imbued with the history of the nation. It carries the history of several nations that use it and this is a factor which may have lent it a flavour of internationality, facilitating this global spread of the language. It is also an eclectic language which borrows heavily from other languages instead of constructing new words for new concepts from inside, from older words by means of derivation and composition. Therefore, English has a very wealthy vocabulary, cumbersomely so at times, meaning that "words for related concepts are typically not related to each other in any obvious, regular manner." This richness of vocabulary may also help make it so appealingly international but at the same time it may prove as a hindrance in international communication because of the difficulty of learning this vocabulary. At the same time, as any language, English has evolved as a spoken language and, thus, encompasses various dialects and forms which, essentially, impede communication.

8.3.3. Resistance to the Dominance of English on the Internet

There are many voices that decry what they consider to be the "hegemony" or the "neocolonialism" of the English language. It is considered that, in an English- dominated communication, English speakers are in a position to control communication to their own advantage. This is in connection with the US-dominated media in general but it is also valid when it comes to the Internet, nowadays, the purveyor by excellence of news and information.

Subsequently, the spread of the English language is viewed as a threat to other languages, having become the alluring language of power and prestige. In the opinion of the experts the current status of the English language on the Internet can only be toppled in two ways: the emergence of the European Union and the rise of a non-existent Chinese-Japanese empire. Both events would involve the birth of a new official language to unite the different nations forming the new powers. Yet, if the formation of the EU results in the creation of an official language, due to the fact that it is a conglomerate of already established nations, it seems to have a purely bureaucratic destination, and it may very well be English.

As to the appearance of a Chinese-Japanese empire—in the wake of the technological and economic boom of the two countries, the choice of a common language seems fraught with difficulties. It too may decide to adopt English as its official language both for continuity's sake but also for the reason that opting for either Chinese or Japanese may very well endanger the union between the two nations. Of course, a valid option for both situations would be the creation of a new, more culturally neutral language.

8.3.4. Controlling the Language of the Internet

Imposing an official language would be a source of control over the Internet but when it was invented, the Internet was not intended for control. Freedom of information is protected under the Universal Declaration of Human Rights and it is enshrined in the US Constitution. It was reinforced by The Council of Europe in 2003 through their Declaration on Freedom of Information on the Internet. Nevertheless, the past two decades, however, have shown that the most treasured possessions of the net—anonymity and unlimited access—have started to show the reverse of the medal. With privacy violations, spamming, hate mail, misinformation and other types of more serious cyber-crime spreading, efforts are being made to curb illegal actions that are so easily perpetrated under the cover of anonymity.

8.3.5. Language in Cyberspace is Changing

What is obvious from observing the language flowing on the Internet is that invariably it is changing. It would be impossible not to, at the fingertips of billions of users from all over the world. But, before analysing those changes, there is another issue that proves to be relevant for communication on the Internet.

8.3.6. Concept of Closeness and Distance

Communication is realised in two ways, referring to the medium: through spoken or written language. There are different degrees of formality associated with both. Communicative closeness is associated with the spoken language whereas written language should be communicatively distant. However, the situation is not that clear-cut. For instance, a letter to a friend is written so far as the medium is concerned yet the concept may be oral whilst a telephone call, oral in medium, may have a distant communication. Therefore, it is safe to say that the degree of formality depends on the recipient of the communication rather than the sender.

The reason this concept is important for communicating on the Internet is that the great bulk of interaction on the net is achieved through a written medium, with chat and email in the place of a telephone conversation, being almost instant. Therefore, the Internet wavers between closeness and distance. Email and chat users may find themselves spatially at a distance but the swiftness of the transmission of any document anywhere in the world negates whatever distance exists between Internet users. The sense of intimacy that is created in this way explains the conceptual orality felt by many that use the net as a medium of communication.

8.3.7. Linguistic Particularities

Internet communication is also spontaneous which also impacts on the language. The typical language on the Internet consists of short and handy words. The lack of any grammatical or stylistic regulation on the Internet has left the door open for the existence of a continuously evolving and dynamic communication. New words are invented at the touch of a button. Some have entered the mainstream, like 'online', 'email', 'e-Bay', 'to google', FAQ, others are being used by a more restricted group of Internet users, like 'netizen' (citizen, user of the net), netcronym (net and acronym). Internet interaction being similar to spoken language, its vocabulary is composed of simple and short words as well as colloquial expressions, onomatopoeia interjections and meaningless phrases, much like in everyday conversation. Being a visual space, the Internet cannot provide extensive, face-to-face communication and everything it involves: facial expressions, gestures, pitch of voice or accent, handing over to someone with a nod, or a wink. In chat rooms, these features have been partially replaced by a very particular strategy: the smileys or Emoticons.

8.3.7.1. Replacing non-verbal communication

The smiley face was invented back at the beginning of the 80s by Scott Fahlman at Carengie Mellon University as stand-ins for the non-verbal communication going on the University's electronic bulletin boards, precursors of today's newsgroups. Due to the fact that attitude could not be transmitted with the written word, various messages intended to be sarcastic, ironic, bored, funny used to be misunderstood, sparking the so called 'flame wars' among users of the bulleting board. The invention of the sideways smiley face, :-), later called emoticon, aimed at appeasing such conflicts, spawned an Internet revolution with hundreds of similar signs appearing soon after.

8.3.7.2. Linguistic mutations

Although the language used in cyberspace is English, the multitude of non-native internauts who all have various levels of knowledge of the language they use means that invariably the language is subject to changes.

Firstly, due to the rapidity, spontaneity and orality of communication via emails, chat rooms, newsgroups, punctuation and captalisation of letters no longer matters. The casualness resulting from the feeling of closeness between users means that typing mistakes are a common occurrence.

Grammatical correction takes a back seat in Internet communication. What is more, a series of phenomena happen, giving rise to new and rapidly adopted words of the youth culture:

- Assimilation (wanna from want to, pics or pix from pictures, thanx instead of thanks)
- Sound alike slang (how R U—how are you, l8ter—later, 4u—for you),
- Ellipses (Sorry, to hear about you situation. Hope you're better).

Word formation already touched upon previously is another interesting and prolific phenomenon that is spreading with the Internet:

- Derivation, through prefixation, suffixation and conversion (e-mail, online, cyberspace, cyber-crime, e-business),
- Compounding (Internet nanny, homepage, website, plug-and-play)
- Blends (emoticon, netcronym, netizen, luser—loser and user, netiquette)
- Acronyms (TLA—Three Letter Acronyms, FAQ—Frequently Asked Questions)
- LOL—Laughing Out Loud, IKWYM—I Know What You Mean

Of course, this is only a fraction of the plethora of transformations affecting the English language on the Internet. And since the community is so impossibly widespread, and, therefore, impossibly hard to control linguistically, there is no sign of the trend stopping or being stopped in the future.

8.4. Reinforcing Old Dominance

Power and dominance are central to "critical pedagogy." Paolo Freire and those involved in critical pedagogy emphasize the need for learning that is personally and socially relevant and that leads to greater self-awareness. Teachers and learners need to realise the power to define who they are, including how they think and communicate. Power inequality is at the heart of concerns about the digital divide. While not everyone may want to be immersed in technology, knowledge about and access to technology are a source of power in today's digital world.

Linguists and language teachers know that change is part of any living language. Each generation of speakers of a language brings its own new words (neologisms) and language styles. Interaction with people from other areas, whether or not they speak the same first language, also means language change. A new ethnic restaurant in a town brings new food vocabulary. Developments in technology, new inventions, new industrial processes—these all add vocabulary.

The BBC is no longer a bastion of British Received Pronunciation; its newscasters display a wide range of dialects. American English has always been based on how people speak, not how they should speak. Reference to an English dictionary means referring to what is commonly in use by the large body of English speakers. What this means is that English has few official, overt constraints on change.

Speakers of English today comprise a very large number of people across the globe. Figures vary, but an estimate that includes both first- and second-language speakers of English is that there are some 1.125 billion people worldwide who use English. Only Chinese surpasses English in the number of speakers. These numbers do not account for how well second-language speakers can actually use the language, however.

Shifting to the Internet, English has been and still is the most commonly-used language online, with nearly double the number of users of Chinese, the second most common language. In terms of number of websites, English also holds sway with over 68% of the total websites around the world in English. In 2007, an estimated 53% of the total Internet addresses issued around the world, and by extension the number of different servers, were in the United States. This gives English, and particularly the US varieties of English, substantial dominance on the Web.

Business email still incorporates polite forms and follows many business letter conventions, though there may not be the same kind of formal opening and closing as in a printed letter. Business email writers are generally quite aware that their messages are, potentially, important documents that could win a promotion or result in being fired. Academic web sites retain many elements of more formal writing, as well, with citations and bibliographies not uncommon. Informal email, personal websites, and most other Internet situations move further from the conventions of formal writing and incorporate more elements of speech. Most importantly, there are currently few widely-accepted conventions governing language use on the Internet. Businesses, schools, chat monitors, and discussion groups set individual standards. Most of these are based on the lowest common denominator, referencing basic "netiquette"and behaviour to avoid.

The most distinct new forms of language seem to be on synchronous channels of communication, such as text-based chat and instant messaging. Chat with multiple simultaneous participants poses a variety of technology- induced challenges for communication. Another technical element that adds to the unusual communication in chat is "lag"—a time delay between when a message is sent by an individual and when it is visible to everyone else. The amount of lag depends on how many people are involved in the chat and on the speed of each individual's connection to the Internet.

One more socio-psychological element is "cyberculture". Strate, et al. call it "The unique culture associated with CMC and online interaction". Cyberculture was originally associated with hackers, and much of it maintains a certain irreverent, playful, and anti-establishment quality. New words, phrases, abbreviations, and emotive spellings are freely coined in this creative atmosphere.

Add wide access internationally to the Internet to this brave new world of largely ungoverned Internet communication, and the possibility for language change becomes very large. Interaction among the peoples of the world is going on today at a previously unimaginable level in speed, quantity, and diversity of people involved.

References

Baron, N., "Letters by phone or speech by other means: The linguistics of email", *Language and Communication*, 1998.

Baron, N.S., *Alphabet to email: How written English evolved and where it's heading*, New York: Routledge, 2000.

Brutt-Griffler, J., *World English: A study of its development*, Clevedon, England: Multilingual Matters, 2002.

Canagarajah, S., *Resisting linguistic imperialism in English teaching*, Oxford, England: Oxford University Press, 1999.

Candlin, C. N., & Mercer, N., *English language teaching in its social contexts: A reader*, London: Routledge, 2001.

Crystal, D., *Language and the Internet*, Cambridge: Cambridge University Press, 2001.

Gao, L., "Language contact and convergence in computer-mediated communication", *World Englishes*, 2006.

Herring, S.C. (Ed.), *Computer-mediated communication: Linguistic, social and cross-cultural perspectives*, Amsterdam: Benjamins, 1996.

Internet World Stats, "Internet world users by language", Available at http://www.internetworldstats.com/stats7.htm, Accessed January 11, 2006.

Kachru, B., "World Englishes and English-using communities", *Annual Review of Applied English*, 1997.

Lee, J.Y., "Charting the codes of cyberspace: A rhetoric of electronic mail", In L. Strate, R.L. Jacobson, and S.B. Gibson (Eds.), *Communication and cyberspace: Social interaction in an electronic environment*, Cresskill, NJ: Hampton Press, 2002.

Li, L., 'Email: A challenge to Standard English?", *English Today*, 2000.

Melchers, G. and Shaw, P., *World Englishes: An introduction*, London: Arnold, 2003.

Rahul Goswami, "Globalization Challenges Asian Languges", *Asia Times Online*, 31 July 2003.

Strate, L., Jacobson, R.L., & Gibson, S.B., "Surveying the electronic landscape: An introduction to Communication and cyberspace", In L. Strate, R.L. Jacobson, and S.B. Gibson (Eds.), *Communication and cyberspace: Social interaction in an electronic environment*, Cresskill, NJ: Hampton Press, 2002.

9

Socio-cultural Issues of Global English

In the dominant Western culture today, traditional ideas of connectedness and togetherness embedded in the concept of community no longer rely upon local contact. Media and multimedia mean that reality and virtual reality now have blurred outlines: they are merging into an eculture. Globalisation means that, for the first time in human history, the nuances of shared meanings are no longer dependent upon geography. This does not mean that the Western world comes to other cultures with an interest in exchange and equality: rather, it subsumes them through electronic colonisation just as it did with geographic colonisation.

Although globalisation may have been an inevitable consequence, it can also be seen as an electronic colonisation, an electronic cultural imperialism. In this way, it is innately destructive towards non-English speaking communities. Globalisation is a centralising influence. Take English as the global language, for example. Despite the resurgence of some languages such as Hebrew, Hawaiian, and Gaelic, most languages—and therefore most communities—are faced with the question of how to continue, much less to thrive, in a globalised world.

As we know, English is *the* global language. This seems pretty simple and convincing at first glance. It is particularly seductive for those of us who speak, listen, think, read, and write in English. We easily accept the idea that technology is such a force that every aspect of life is undergoing change because of it and the binary of real/reality and hyper-real/virtual reality is being bridged via the English language. In cyberspace most of their languages, the workshops of their culture, are subsumed into the new global language: English. Thus a new cultural and linguistic "reality" is built.

9.1. Global Equality

Access to power in the eGlobal is clearly as unequal as access to power in the geographic global itself. In Albania, there are 3.45 million people and 12,000 Internet users compared with 3 million in the Congo and 500 users, the United States with 280.5 million and 182.13 million users, and a similar percentage in the United Kingdom of 59.8 million population with 34.3 million users.

Similarly, the geographic starting and reception points for Internet activities show just how restricted the eGlobal is in practice. Most of the traffic is from the American major cities to the major British and European ones. The traffic shows that the borderless ideal of the eGlobal is not apparent in reality. Just as in real geographic space those of us who are already enabled are further enabled in cyberspace. eGlobal interactions on the Internet indicate that most users are from a particular geographic space and a particular demographic. As in the geographic world, the most prominent subtextual influence on the eGlobal is the dominant ideology of the Western culture: late capitalism. Clearly, the eGlobal means something totally different in the Congo or Albania from what it means in the U.S.A or the U.K. Such evidence shows that any ideal of a cyber world with access for all is unlikely to be sustained. In fact, eGlobal culture and meaning in both its text and subtext are produced in our society by powerful Western and Western-oriented money-makers largely through dominance of the media.

9.2. Economic, Military, Political and Technological Issues

The cluster of economic, military, political, and technological factors that led to the worldwide dominance of English as a language of wider communication is well documented. Over a decade ago, this process to the role English plays in encoding technological information and permitting access to that information. English was a prerequisite for any individuals or societies expecting to compete in the international marketplace. Technology and especially of the Internet, and a growing perception that trade and other international exchanges were reaching hitherto unaffected regions of the globe. All of this—for better or worse—reflected an American worldview and favoured its main carrier, English.

For the small minority whose professional lives—and with them, their continued access to prosperity and power—require that they be part of international exchanges, English is key. In a rare and useful attempt at quantifying perceptions of language dominance in terms of number of speakers, geographic distribution, and ratio of speakers to per capita GNP, English leaves far behind other languages of wider communication (past and present) such as Dutch, German, Italian, Hindi, Japanese, Portuguese, and Russian but also more often mentioned competitors such as Arabic, Chinese, French, and Spanish. Clearly, perceptions of relative strength can be highly unstable, and a week can be a long time in geopolitics, as the events of September 2001 and the rapid rearrangement of alliances that followed amply demonstrated. However, given the current privileged position of English, it is reasonable to assume that it would take long-term socioeconomic disruption on a scale far more catastrophic than that brought about by those attacks on symbols of US supremacy for the cluster of factors that gave rise to the dominance of English to unravel and for the role of English as a global language to be seriously threatened in the near future.

No language has ever had so many speakers and played such a broad range of roles, locally as well as internationally. Although some useful parallels can be drawn between the diffusion of Latin through sizable areas of Europe as a result of the geopolitical expansion of its Roman base, this phenomenon is only of limited relevance to the current spread of English, in part because the process went largely unrecorded and is therefore difficult to trace. More importantly, the diffusion of Latin and the linguistic indigenisation and split that followed were not constrained by the standardising forces operating through modern language planning agencies, the print media, and, in an increasingly literate world, public education. Only much later did Latin usage come to feel the effect of standardisation as a result of the stable nature of the religious content it carried and the strongly centralising tendencies of the Catholic Church. Nor is the role until relatively recently of Latin as a lingua franca in parts of the western world likely to be much of a guide because it remained the preserve of small professional elites, far removed in nature from the large numbers that today take part in interethnic and supranational communication involving some variety of English or other.

In the event of such a shift in geopolitical circumstances, the dominant language associated with that emerging power would first have to arrest and then reverse the advantage English now derives from critical mass. To do this, a global challenger would need to benefit from three key factors. Firstly, it would need to possess a set of linguistic characteristics that would facilitate its acquisition as a second language by individuals with largely instrumental motivations. Among these characteristics are minimal inflectional morphology, non-tonal phonology, and a non-logographic script. Secondly, to have a better chance of evolving such a set of favourable characteristics if it did not possess them already, a language with worldwide ambition would need to benefit from weak political and administrative control over form and usage and enjoy the freedom to accommodate unplanned, user-driven change leading to both structural simplification and a degree of creolisation as the language adapts to local conditions in amultiplicity of sociolinguistic settings. Finally, a language competing for global prominence would have to be perceived—rightly or wrongly—as carrying the kind of sociocultural content and economic promise likely to .re the imagination of potential users and motivate them to undertake the task of learning the language, a challenge of some magnitude to most adult learners.

In practice, regardless of their sociocultural or linguistic characteristics and despite large populations of native speakers, most languages that might hypothetically compete with English for a global role are likely to remain closely tied to a political or economic entity with little chance of achieving significant socioeconomic prominence beyond their regional base or their ethnic diaspora in the foreseeable future. The list of languages matching this description is a long one, and inclusion or omission is to some extent subjective and potentially controversial. Certainly, the combination of sheer numbers of speakers and current socioeconomic conditions suggests that the list might include—but by no means be limited to —languages such as Bengali, Hindi, Kiswahili, Malay, and Portuguese.

9.3. Global Potential

A proposition running through writings on the worldwide spread of English holds that languages of wider communication prosper or wither according to the amount of information they contain. Thus Sanskrit, Chinese, Greek, Arabic, Latin, French, and German all served—and in some cases, continue to serve—as depositories of privileged information—be it religious, legal, or technological—and as vehicles for the transmission and expansion of that information. Today, for a growing number of users, English functions as depository and transmitter of information related not only to science and technology but also, like its predecessors, to broader economic and cultural exchanges.

Clearly, English is not the only language currently fulfilling this kind of role. Languages can be seen as forming part of a global system consisting of several major constellations, each with its own set of local languages related to one central language, namely, the one spoken by the most multilinguals within the constellation. Some ten or twelve constellations can be readily identified. Some map fairly closely onto national borders and those of immediate neighbours. Some, such as French or Portuguese, link an erstwhile colonial power and its former dependencies despite territorial separation, while others connect a dominant group in a large, socially complex country with other linguistic groups within the country and with a widely scattered diaspora (eg, Hindi or Chinese). One of the less often mentioned languages operating in this fashion is Urdu, a language for which Aziz makes a plea, arguing that it should be taught in South Africa as a language of cross-cultural communication, to strengthen links between that country and the Indian sub-continent, and to foster mutual tolerance and understanding.

Other languages of this type are Malay—in both its Bahasa Melayu and Bahasa Indonesia varieties—and Bengali, both spoken by more speakers than German or Japanese, presumably because of the relatively minor geopolitical roles played by the nations with which they are associated. Within each constellation, the communicative potential of the dominant language is a factor of its prevalence as a mother tongue and its spread among multilinguals. This is an advantageous situation that the elites in charge of their respective sphere of influence are unlikely to relinquish, especially since maintaining this advantage becomes easier as nations grow wealthier.

Thus, while English competes with Hindi in India and with Spanish and French in North America, it is now essentially without competitor at the global level, except perhaps in international organisations such as the United Nations or the European Union that continue to reflect earlier geopolitical realities. By now, it is likely that the dominant position of English has become a self-reinforcing process. English is growing in supranational reach not only in direct relation to the amount of information it contains but also because the more people choose to learn it in one part of the world, the more attractive it becomes in other communities, exponentially.

A key ingredient in the process of self-expansion is critical mass, the point at which sheer number of speakers, their wide geographic distribution, and their sociopolitical and economic power makes it too costly for a competitor to enter the fray. As in all monopolistic situations, lack of competition blunts incentives and inertia becomes a dominant characteristic of participants in the monopoly, be they providers or consumers. These circumstances probably already apply to speakers of English as their first language, who may see no benefit in making the effort to learn a second language. But it may increasingly apply to potential users of languages of international communication, who may see no reason to challenge the dominant global language since they typically have few emotional ties with that or any other supranational language.

9.3.1. Linguistic Structure

While the critical mass increasingly favouring English alters the dynamics obtaining across linguistic constellations and raises the bar for potential challengers, a number of linguistic factors also allow predictions to be made regarding their eventual success. In principle, all languages have the potential to fulfill any communicative role. In practice, languages are shaped to some extent by their context of use. Like all natural organisms, languages consist of a set of characteristics evolving slowly over time, partly randomly and partly in response to changes in the communicative needs of their speakers as these rearrange themselves geographically and socially. For example, the inflectional complexity of languages such as Icelandic or Finnish is clearly no impediment to the learning of these languages by young children born among a stable population, and thus is under no pressure from within to change in the direction of greater morphological simplicity. However, in the (highly unlikely) event of geopolitical circumstances turning such a language into a contender for a global role, it would surely come under pressure from without to simplify or see current and potential users favour better adapted—that is, easier to master —competitors.

To be sure, modern languages do not evolve entirely as a result of uncontrollable environmental forces. Just as modern humans have gradually gained a sufficient degree of control over their circumstances for reproductive success to no longer be determined by adaptive reactions to raw environmental forces, modern societies have devised institutional tools that allow them to generate and steer change in both language form and language use, with some success as regards writing conventions though generally far less in other areas. Moreover, there is no denying that English owes its current dominant position in large part to historical and geopolitical forces, not primarily linguistic ones. However, it can be argued that the metamorphosis of English from a regional to global role was facilitated by the fact that the language had already undergone a process of linguistic change, leaving it with a set of linguistic characteristics that made subsequent adaptive change less traumatic. By this token, a challenger for the role of dominant global language would have to either possess a set of linguistic characteristics that would make the transition to that role less structurally disruptive or be allowed to evolve one thanks to minimal interference from institutional standardising forces.

The degree of complexity of this set of linguistic characteristics matters because learners of both first and second languages are attentive to a number of competing linguistic cues in their search for form-meaning connections and in their attempt to discover patterns in the input. Among these cues are morphological inflection, tonality, and word order. While identifying and decoding each of these cues presents a special kind of difficulty, facing all of them at once in a hypothetical new language would present learners with an insurmountable cognitive challenge and make that language unlearnable. In practice, unlike young children, most learners of languages of supranational communication tend to be motivated by instrumental objectives. To be sure, there is evidence that second languages—including one with relatively complex inflectional morphology such as Spanish—can be learned to a high level of accuracy even by older learners. For the majority, however, a late start militates against the learning of complex linguistic structure to anything approaching native like standard. It is true that the complex inflectional morphology of French did not prevent language learning success among pre-revolutionary Russian aristocrats, for example. However, the majority of modern users of languages of supranational communication do not share the social and educational privileges that made this kind of proficiency possible among a small elite with ample time and leisure to learn the finer details of a second language, just as earlier elites succeeded—more or less—in mastering the finer points of Latin.

Thus, all other things being equal, it can be predicted that learners of second languages—and especially adult learners—will favour a linguistic compromise offering maximal communicative benefit in return for minimal learning investment to the extent that any complexity beyond the scope of that investment will be ignored if subsequently encountered. In this sense, the structure of any potential language of supranational communication comes under the same pressure that leads to the morphosyntactic minimalism characteristic of pidgins. Indeed, McArthur predicts that the remaining inflectional irregularities of English are likely to be ironed out as the language grows in global significance. McArthur even recommends that the process be hastened, especially in print, through deliberate language policy. In a similar vein, Jenkins offers some guidelines on a pronunciation of English that could be taught across cultures and first language backgrounds with broad mutual intelligibility as the primary objective. In this, both McArthur and Jenkins echo numerous earlier proposals for the rationalisation of the language, several of which are reviewed in Yano.

How, then, does the competition—both hypothetical and probable —stack up against English in this respect? In this sense at least, paucity of inflectional markings gives Chinese an advantage for a future global role for the language. Japanese, meanwhile, does encode tense and marks semantic relationships with a range of affixes and, although there is no reliable means of calculating inflectional complexity, it is probably roughly in the same range of inflectional complexity as English, whose residual inflectional morphology leads many second language learners to comment favourably about its relative ease of learning, at least initially. By contrast, the complex inflectional morphology of Spanish and French presents learners with a substantial challenge. In Spanish, a verb such as *escríbir* has no fewer than 48 possible inflections in various combinations of person, number, tense, and affect, whereas the equivalent English verb has just five forms. Similarly, many learners of Spanish or French adjectives have to contend with four possible forms that reflect gender and number as well as an inherent (prenominal) versus non-inherent distinction.

In contrast, English adjectives come with no inflectional markings and normally modify nouns in prenominal position only. Arabic, German, and Russian, for their part, add a range of case markings to the challenge of encoding meaning in nouns and adjectives. Admittedly, some of these markings—including several of the 48 forms of a common Spanish verb—belong to literary registers and are not likely to be of concern to most users of these languages for purposes of supranational communication. Yet, for the learner aiming for a modicum of accuracy, the difference in the magnitude of the learning task is striking. In theory, this should leave Esperanto with little competition given the care taken by its creators to regularise its form to an extent unattainable by natural languages. However, two difficulties immediately arise.

Firstly, were the language to spread and indigenise in a variety of settings, the price of greater diffusion would most likely be loss of uniformity and a gradual increase in morphological variation. Secondly, the worldwide adoption of Esperanto is made unlikely by its strongly European nature. To speakers of non-European languages who constitute a substantial proportion of its potential customer base, the language looks remarkably similar to the obvious and economically more attractive alternative, namely English. To these potential users, not having to master the mildly irritating inflectional irregularities of English would be meager compensation for being shut out—at least initially—of existing global networks. The likely outcome is that these potential users will prefer a European language with which they are already familiar (English) over a quasi-European language with which they are not (Esperanto).

A second linguistic factor likely to affect the supranational potential of specific languages is phonology, and in particular the issue of tonality. Although the acquisition of a tonal language obviously presents no insurmountable problems for first language learners, it is reportedly very difficult when tackled by learners in adulthood. This leaves all the hypothetical challengers to English under consideration here evenly matched except for Chinese since it relies on tonal differences to create semantic contrasts. Although auditory training can be effective in the identification and retention of Chinese tones by adult learners, tone perception and production is especially difficult for these learners. As in all cases of language-in-contact accommodation, the likely consequence is a degree of structural simplification, namely, some tone loss in the international variety of Chinese that would evolve as a result of the global spread of the language and its use by an increasing number of non-native speakers, a scenario supported by evidence from a range of African and Asian tonal languages. Since coping with tonality would require additional training relative to non-tonal competitors and strain the limited resources of potential learners, tonality appears to constitute something of a handicap for Chinese as a potential language of international communication.

9.3.2. Writing Systems

An additional factor likely to influence the chances of hypothetical challengers to English as a global language is the writing system favoured by each language. Clearly, a challenger would have to meet the needs of large numbers of literate users under pressure to communicate at a distance and with relatively limited resources to devote to learning the language. This raises the question of the suitability of a primarily logographic writing system such as the one used by Chinese and, with adaptations, Japanese.

Although the Chinese script can be said to be primarily logographic, it also—and contrary to widespread misperceptions—incorporates a phonemic element. It is primarily logographic in that key semantic components (known as "radicals") stand for meaning without the intermediary step of representing the phonology encoding that meaning and despite the fact that very few symbol-meaning relationships can be said to be iconic. However, Chinese script also incorporates a phonemic element in that radicals are typically combined with characters that stand for words with similar pronunciation but no semantic connection. Constraints apply to possible combinations of radicals and phonemic components, their location in relation to each other, and stroke direction for both. In addition, and also contrary to popular belief, progress in acquiring the system is not achieved by rote but through a growing understanding of the rules underlying the system. While children aged six are normally competent at handling the key semantic radicals, three more years of study are required for competence in the use of phonological components of the script.

All of these factors in addition to the number of combinations that need to be mastered explain why the system is widely regarded as comparatively difficult to learn—though relatively easy to decipher once learned—and why learning and teaching a script of this type to a standard permitting communication across a wide range of subjects and registers constitutes an onerous task, both cognitively and educationally. Moreover, the fact that the system is only partially phonemic largely rules out self-access through reading as a major route to language learning—at least in the early stages—and makes the acquisition of lexis heavily dependent on teachers and other native or native like speakers.

Computers are increasingly accommodating of logographic writing, the future generalisation of speech recognition technologies is unlikely to facilitate the decoding of the logographic component of the script even if it reduces encoding difficulties. Overall, learning this type of script is not a task that instrumentally driven users of a language of international communication are likely to take up readily if a less resource-hungry alternative exists.

Most likely, that alternative will be a script based primarily on the representation of phonemic segments. Although this alternative could in principle be either alphabetic or syllabic depending on the phonotactic structure of the language in question, the range of hypothetical languages of supranational communication under consideration here rules out the syllabic option unless Japanese were to abandon the primarily logographic kanji script and rely entirely on one of its two kana syllabaries. This would leave Esperanto with a clear lead given its close match between pronunciation and script characteristic of all artificial languages.

Meanwhile, English, French, German, and Spanish would be evenly matched, though German and Spanish do have the advantage of a script that has remained closer to pronunciation over the centuries, at least as regards the standard variety of these languages. Although a global role for Russian and Arabic may be somewhat hampered by their association with scripts shared by few other languages, the alphabetic nature of these scripts would not in principle be a major obstacle.

9.3.3. Standardisation

A related factor likely to affect the potential of hypothetical languages of supranational communication is their degree of exposure to standardising forces. Ideologically unwelcome though the notion might seem to many, the idea of promoting a standard across varieties of a language does have some supporters. In theory at least, supranational standards guarantee a degree of egalitarianism among all speakers of an international variety. In the context of English, Bamgbose argues, non-native communities of speakers are at risk of even greater disadvantage in that the very absence of standardisation for new Englishes risks encouraging these varieties to continue looking to established varieties for exonormative standards Yet, however desirable a degree of standardisation may be in some circumstances, it can be argued that the internationalisation of English has been facilitated by the accidental combination of two favourable factors. Not only is English largely free of the kinds of inflectional complexities that would strain the resources of instrumentally motivated potential users and rapidly come under pressure for spontaneous simplification in a supranational context.

Today, the dominant view of English as a global language emphasizes the range of its varieties operating as an interconnected system, each variety closely related to a relatively stable core and infinitely adaptable in its own localised setting.

Resistance to supranational standardisation is also a factor of the peculiar geographic distribution of English born of the growing geopolitical reach of speakers of the language. What started as limited maritime trade and the westward migration of a few thousand people from a small island off. Western Europe resulted in a language now distributed among a number of power centers, each with its own sociocultural characteristics and its own set of regional and global interconnections. While the present-day dominance of the North American variety is undeniable, history as well as a literary canon that continues to command worldwide attention is likely to give the British variety lasting influence. Despite its narrower range, the Australian variety is unlikely to be challenged within its own regional sphere of influence. Much the same is true of India because of its large population, the power it wields regionally, and the fact that the variety serves to tie the component parts of India to each other and the whole to neighbours that share a common colonial history.

As a result, it is now unimaginable that one of these varieties—even the American variety —would come to command so much more sociolinguistic clout than any of the others that it could—deliberately or accidentally—exert sufficient gravitational force as to reduce related varieties to minor variants of itself. This division into several relatively equal, or at least culturally autonomous and selfconfident poles, and the resulting multi-core distribution of modern English are likely to continue making the language resistant to standardisation.

Considered independently of other factors, the wide distribution of Arabic across national borders should in principle make that language at least as impervious to standardisation as English. This should ensure that no single variety dominates and that the language is permitted to adapt to local environments while maintaining sufficient unity to function as a language of international communication. However, this potential for adaptation is reduced by the close association of the language with a religious message that does not lend itself readily to relativistic interpretations. As a result, the potential for Arabic to adapt to local settings, especially in its written—hence most easily standardised—form and to take on a global role must be regarded as limited, even if other geopolitical factors were favourable.

For its part, Spanish has a long and well-documented history of attempts at standardisation through the publication of grammars and dictionaries that often aimed to resist the alleged superiority of French norms. Today, attitudes to the international role of Spanish and to internal variation are more utilitarian and relaxed than French ones, no doubt owing to the early weakening of Spanish imperial power and the resulting independence from Spain of relatively isolated nations, as well as to contact within many of these nations with a range of indigenous languages. Although the Spanish Academy has a fearsome history of watching over language standards as far as its reach will allow, the huge demographic imbalance between Spain and the Spanish-speaking Americas means that any standardisation in Spanish today is more likely to come semi-haphazardly from US-based TV networks broadcasting to the entire continent than from an ancient European planning agency. Thus, geopolitical and economic considerations apart, a combination of the multi-core distribution of modern Spanish, the relative ineffectiveness of centrally-directed standardisation, and weak resistance to indigenisation give Spanish an advantage in these hypothetical global language stakes.

Several of the other potential competitors under consideration here are tied to a single culture that is massively dominant within a single nationwith only an increasingly detached diaspora to support it internationally. Two languages of this type are Japanese and German, both closely associated with countries that for historical reasons remain reluctant to assert themselves culturally or politically. Certainly, unlike English, neither has experienced the kind of linguistic or cultural schism triggered by a former dependency going its own way while retaining the language of the former colonial power. Although Japanese functioned as a supranational language for only a brief period in Taiwan and to some extent in Korea and China, no new nation has risen or looks likely to rise from within the Japanese-speaking fold to threaten the unquestioned standardising tendencies of the center. This puts Japanese at a disadvantage as regards its suitability as a potential language of wider communication.

As for German, a degree of ambivalence toward standardisation can be seen in the failure of recent attempts by the German authorities to enact spelling reform. From the start, this effort ran into fierce debate and even legal action, reflecting the fact that 75% of the population opposed the reform, which was eventually abandoned unilaterally by leading newspapers. In the sense that institutional standardising forces thus appear relatively weak, the language seems relatively well adapted to the unavoidable pressure for morphological simplification that would inevitably follow its hypothetical international spread. Somewhat more internationalised is Russian, with its history of pre-revolutionary and Soviet-era imperialism and of close control—including linguistic control—over the affairs of its immediate neighbours. Yet, Russia has an unremarkable record of linguistic spread despite having recently wielded considerable geopolitical power as far a field as in Angola, Cuba, or Vietnam. Moreover, no Russian-speaking nation has ever emerged or looks likely to emerge to challenge the standardising power of the Russian heartland.

China has so far managed to keep its core domain territorially intact thanks in part to a pragmatic approach to regional variation. To be sure, sizable portions of the country speak versions of Chinese that by many measures could be described as distinct languages were it not for the demands of political expediency. This factor, along with the role played by primarily logographic writing among an increasingly literate population, leads to the convenient fiction that Chinese constitutes a single language and that all teaching in China—except that of indigenous languages—takes place in the preferred Mandarin standard. Meanwhile, issues of standardisation affect mainly the treatment of linguistic imports—especially in the field of technology —and continuing discussions of the issue of romanisation.

Clearly, despite major variation within China as well as across China and a widely dispersed Chinese diaspora, and despite increasingly overt Taiwanese attempts at establishing a degree of communal identity and linguistic autonomy, no threat is currently visible to the official dominance of standard Mandarin. On the surface, there is no doubt where authority in matters of the Chinese language is meant to reside. However, given the fact that standardisation is in part cosmetic, Chinese does have the potential to adapt to multiple settings successfully were China to accede to global power status. French, meanwhile, has a long history of deliberate standardisation that parallels the centralising policies of successive regimes and governments and the promotion of a linguistic standard on the basis of its allegedly superior nature in terms of clarity and rationality.

Over the past two centuries especially, the imposition of standard French constituted a key strategy for the elimination of social, political, and religious ideologies regarded as reactionary and for the promotion of revolutionary concepts such as egalitarianism. This long-standing concern with implementing political ideals and objectives through language policy explains modern French concerns about perceived threats to national unity and a preoccupation with linguistic purity. Today, this acceptance of a key role for the institutions of the state in defining and safeguarding cultural values along with their linguistic embodiment leads many influential French commentators to regard the ability of English to absorb input from many sources as commercially motivated and therefore suspect. In addition, French has long been inextricably tied to a historically, politically, economically, and culturally dominant territorial core. With other French-speaking or partially French-speaking communities either located in economically or politically dependent countries (mostly in Africa) or constituting linguistic minorities within larger countries (Canada, Belgium, Switzerland), this unbalanced geographic distribution serves the centralising tendencies of the core and makes it less likely that the language will be allowed the freedom to develop organically into an ever-adaptable tool of global communication.

9.3.4. Modernisation

In a rapidly changing world, access to knowledge is no longer a luxury enjoyed by a tiny leisured class sitting at the apex of a feudal society. Today, it is a major predictor of which members of a society are likely to see tangible improvement in their standard of living and which are likely to stay poor. Admittedly, knowledge comes in many forms and is carried by many linguistic vehicles. In developing societies especially, such thinking and learning is likely to lead to an interest in what might be termed "big ideas" such as democratic participation and civil rights and to a turn of mind favouring inquiry, criticism, and skepticism.

In practice, however, it is important to recall that the import of values and of the languages that encode them can just as often be the consequence—as opposed to the root cause—of major changes in local mindsets and developmental objectives. For example, when the Chinese leadership decided in 1986 that the market route to economic development was likely to yield greater rewards than the earlier centrally-planned experiment, it committed itself —unwittingly, no doubt—to importing notions that had not been part of earlier arrangements governing business or public administration. Among these are corporate governance, conflict of interest, transparency, and disclosure, all of which are essential to the successful conduct of large-scale business, especially in a globalised context.

The test of English or any other international conveyor of modernising and liberating notions is not that it introduces values regarded as foreign and therefore either good or bad in some abstract sense. It is whether these values help to bring about beneficial change in the form of generalised wealth creation benefiting most in a less hierarchical society. Interest in these values is no pro-western fad. They appeal because they are seen as helping to understand the relative economic success of western societies, where they were first given a chance. For as long as these values are regarded as preferable to traditional, home-grown ones and for as long as they are strongly associated with English-speaking cultures, any challenge to English as a vehicle for these values is unlikely to succeed.

Though undeniably a much-respected language of wider communication in fields that include the creative arts, Arabic remains strongly associated with Islam, a religion that structures the existence of its followers in clear-cut terms through an especially inelastic set of tenets. In addition, the transmission of this time-honoured religious and societal knowledge tends to take place through rote-learning encoded in Arabic, a foreign language for large numbers of followers of Islam in Central Asia, Iran, the Indian sub-continent, sub-Saharan Africa, or Indonesia. There, reliance on repetition of a poorly-understood language may have the effect of associating that language with knowledge that is remote and therefore not amenable to questioning. Intentionally or otherwise, this may discourage the development of a culture of exegesis, criticism, and skepticism, the very values singled out by Prabhu as most likely to recommend a language as a vehicle for modernisation and liberation.

In principle, the potential of Japanese as a international language suffers from few if any of the cultural restrictions described above. In fact, throughout the 1980s, Japan was regarded as the primary source of all things new and beautiful in three areas: electronic technology, business practices, and consumer fads. In the more prosperous parts of the world at least, few lives have been untouched by some Japanese invention or concept, from the fax or the walkman on the consumer side to Just-In-Time Delivery or Zero-Defect Manufacturing in the business world and *manga* strip cartoons or *Pokémon* on the cultural side. Yet, despite deliberate governmental policy to promote the teaching of Japanese as a second language, the language does not appear to have progressed far beyond the level of a school subject or to have made significant inroads as a tool for regional, let alone worldwide communication.

References

Barr, T., *The changing face of Australia's media and communications,* Sidney, Australia: Allen and Unwin, 2000.

Braudel, F., *Civilization and Capitalism 15th-18th century,* London, UK: William Collins and Sons, 1983.

Baudrillard, J., *The violence of the global,* (F. Debrix, Trans.) Paris: Galilee, 2002.

Spivak, G., *A critique of postcolonial reason,* Cambridge, MA: Harvard University, 2000.

10

Global English and Progressive Struggle

Philippe Van Parijs argues that English should be adopted as Europe's lingua franca because we do not want Europeanisation, and beyond it globalisation, to be the exclusive preserve of the wealthy and the powerful who can afford quality interpretation. If we want all sorts of workers', women's, young people's, old people's, poor people's associations to organise on the every higher scale required for effective action, we must equip them with the means of talking to one another without the need for interpreting boxes and the highly skilled and paid professionals who go in them.

This is perhaps one of the most important arguments in favour of global English from a social justice perspective. As we shall see, it mirrors Gramsci's argument about the need for a truly common national Italian language in the early 20Century. But, unlike Gramsci, for Van Parijs, this position is part of an analysis of European language politics premised on individualistic and rational-choice presumptions or methodology. But in contrast to other ration-choice individualists, Van Parijs highlights the detrimental effects of the use of English as a lingua franca. He is most concerned about the linguistic injustice in that language as a common good is 'paid for' both literally and figuratively very disproportionately by non-English first language speakers, but it is first language English speakers who benefit as much or more from this 'common good'. Thus, for him, it is a classic 'free rider' problem and he specifically presents strategies for ameliorating these injustices. In essence, he argues that it is fully possible to compensate for the unfairness created by the "countless uncoordinated choices" which have selected English as the world's lingua franca.

For example, Van Parijs suggests that the dubbing of movies and television should be banned based on evidence that the original audio with subtitles helps audiences learn the original languages which is especially likely to be English given the prominence of English-language television and movies. He also proposes subsidies across language groups based on cost-benefit analysis of English as a 'public good'. In addition, he highlights that there are some disadvantages that native English speakers have such as not having a 'private' language nor having as good opportunities to learn new languages. But regardless of his concerns with the injustice of 'global English', his analysis serves to highlight the problems involved with conceptualising language as being primarily communicative.

Van Parijs begins with two basic propositions. The first is that "The extent to which people maintain and improve their linguistic competence in some particular language" is a matter of 'motivation' caused by the usefulness of competence and the 'opportunity' to actually use the language. He labels this probability that an individual language learner will 'have to' function in the new language, "probability-sensitive learning". The second is what he calls the "maximin law of communication" – the notion that the abstract individual "will systematically tend to ask yourself whether there is any language that is known to some extent by all" of those you want to communicate with. In other words, speakers will try to maximise the minimum competence within their audiences.

He argues that "*as soon as* efficiency in communication prevails over pedagogical or expressive concerns, perceptible inequalities in the minimum knowledge of the various languages involved will generate a hardly resistible pressure for all to adopt the maximin language". Van Parijs offers us an explicit division between the communicative dimensions of language and the symbolic dimensions. To this common division, Van Parijs adds a 'pedagogical' or 'didactic' dimension. Again, in a relatively common procedure, Van Parijs uses these distinctions in order to de-emphasise the 'symbolic' and 'pedagogical' dimensions, and focus solely on language as a vehicle for communication, "Hence, although didactic effectiveness and symbolic impact may sometimes strongly constrain language choice, this will not prevent the maximin criterion from running the show whenever communication is the prime concern, i.e. in the bulk of spoken and written language use". This is a more systematic example of perhaps the most common assumptions that enables liberal individualist perspectives to grapple with the complexities of language usage.

The abstract individualistic approaches of Van Parijs and De Swaan, certainly cannot explain the 'standardisation' of national languages and demotion of vernacular and dialects throughout Europe from the seventeenth to the twentieth centuries that involved massive state involvement and national mandatory education systems. Thus, to sustain their positions, either normative or empirical, it would have to be shown how the relationship between language and political identity has or should substantially shift in such a way that language is primarily a means of communication separate from being intimately tied to political and cultural identity.

Van Parijs' approach to language politics is very different from that of Abram De Swaan, in that he focuses on the normative dimensions, but they share a central feature. In order to endorse the spread of 'global English' both separate this communicative dimension from other central aspects of language and then down play these other aspects. Because Van Parijs accepts an explicitly normative approach, his separation of these various aspects of language, namely the communicative from any others, can be viewed as a normative desire. Van Parijs to show how to overcome the effects of what Gramsci will call the imposition of a 'normative grammar' of global English.

De Swaan precisely takes a more objective and empirical approach. In his wide-ranging study, *Words of the World,* Abram De Swaan concludes that "a single coherent world language system has emerged; at its core is hypercentral English, which is linked to a dozen supercentral languages... the world language system now connects all known languages in a strongly ordered, strongly connected, hierarchical, four-tiered pattern". He argues that the "hypercentral position of English at the hub of the world language system is not just self-perpetuating, it is self-expanding". He is very clear that a simplistic notion of what Graddol calls 'English triumphalism' is not adequate for understanding the current state of world language usage. Despite this, his assumptions, and the fact that they remain assumptions and not political ideals, lead to a de-politicisation of language and in effect to 'English triumphalism'.

De Swaan applies Immanual Wallerstein's notion of a 'world system' to the realm of language and various language constellations throughout the world. He attempts to map the relation of languages and their speakers to one another categorising them as 'peripheral languages', central or 'planetary languages', 'supercentral languages' and then the category made up only by English, the 'hypercentral language'. He adds to this world systems theory of language model a quantitative and rational choice theory approach to analyse why people choose to learn the languages they do. Working through economic concepts, he defines language as a 'hypercollective good' and then applies a quantitative measure of a Q-value to each language.

The Q-value is the measure of the communicative potential of a language, or the language repertoire of an individual. So it is an attempt to go beyond just measuring a language by the number of speakers who use or know it, or learned it as a mother tongue. Rather a Q-value is "the product of the proportion of those who speak it among all speakers in [their language] constellation *and* the proportion of multilingual speakers whose repertoire includes the language among all multilingual speakers in the constellation". Thus, he wants to provide a more detailed map of how individuals can be related to one another through mutually understandable languages. De Swaan describes this current state in the "evolution of human language" as "blind process" resulting from the "unintended consequences of a myriad of individual decisions (and non-decisions, resignation and compliance) ...".

Similarly, Van Parijs argued that "countless uncoordinated choices" which have selected English as the world's lingua franca. Brutt-Griffler's account is much more nuanced argument that "Imperialism is only the unwitting, even unwilling, *instrument* of the spread of English". But for each, this conclusion rests substantially on their initial assumptions that the communicative aspect of language can be easily separated from, and held as primary over, its other dimensions.

While De Swaan is at pains to emphasise that his analysis is not just about English, but about the make-up of the constellation of languages and how they interact within a world language system, he presumes that individuals choose the language they wish to learn based on its Q-value. It may indeed seem very counter-intuitive since most individuals are given very limited choices about what languages they can learn. Moreover, the variations between a child of immigrant parents 'choosing' the level at which to learn and use her family's language versus that of the larger society, a student choosing among a small set of languages to learn in school and a business person choosing to take classes to improve or learn English take place only after a myriad of policy and educational questions that occur not at the individual level but at the social and especially the governmental level.

De Swaan addresses this problem in a similar way that rational choice theory generally does. He argues that as a generalisation its proof is seen in the outcome. As he states early in his book, "Whether [the Q-value] is an empirically valid construct will appear from subsequent chapters that discuss factual language constellations. If it works, it is real". But this approach has two very real consequences for de-politicising language, making it seem as if changes in language usage are 'natural' or not connected to systemic issues of economic and political power or cultural prestige and identity. First, it de-emphasises the roles of states in having specific policies concerning language education and the like that have been well documented by scholars such as Robert Phillipson and others. Second, it presents language as solely a question of communication separating it from issues of political identity, symbolic and cultural community.

10.1. Language Politics and Standardisation

Antonio Gramsci's conception of 'hegemony' has been influential in the way of understanding and analysing how dominant groups exert their power through the organisation of consent and acquiescence to their power. His concepts have been widely utilised across the social sciences and humanities including discussions of 'global English' as noted above. While Gramsci is known as a working class leader, theorist of culture and prisoner of Italian fascism, what is less well known is that he was also keenly interested in Italian language politics and standardisation.

Gramsci attacked the strategy for 'standardising Italian' at the end of the 19th Century advocated by Alessandro Manzoni, the renowned author of *I promessi sposi (The Betrothed).* Manzoni was appointed to the head of a government commission on unifying Italy linguistically in 1868, just 7 years after the political unification of Italy. His strategy was to adopt the dialect of Florence, especially that of the bourgeoisie, as the model for 'standard' Italian, to be used for dictionaries and grammar books. Moreover, Manzoni proposed that school teachers for all of Italy should be recruited from Tuscany, or as close to Florence as possible. This would enable school children from Sicily to Venetia to be taught a 'common Italian'. In a fascinating comparison that may have made Manzoni roll over in his grave, Gramsci compared Manzoni's strategy to Esperanto. He argued that this language that was supposed to be a 'common national language' would be as artificial and imposed, especially for those farther from Tuscany, such as southern Italy, Sicily and Sardinia.

As early as 1918, drawing on the linguistic arguments of G. I. Ascoli, Gramsci argued that this strategy would be ineffective as there would be continual pressure exerted by what Ascoli called the 'linguistic substratum' –that is the existing dialects – that would alter this supposed 'standard' language. As we shall see, this argument has significant parallels with Braj Kachru's approach to world Englishes focusing on how English is changed. This is what Kachru calls the 'nativisation' of English.

Part of Gramsci's political and cultural critique of Manzoni's method is comparable to critics of 'global English' who note that language is tied to culture and ways of understanding the world, so that the use, adoption or imposition of a 'foreign' language includes values and beliefs as well as questions of inferiority and prestige of speakers' identities. Kachru extends this to argue that English is an Asian language and becomes fully capable of expressing various different Asian values and identities *because* it is altered. So he is not arguing that because language is a neutral vehicle for communication, as an empty conduit, it can be filled with any set of values and identities. Kachru argued that 'Asian Englishes' are 'Asian' languages in that they contain Asian values, identity and distinct possibilities of creativity. This notion that language can not be properly understood by making its communicative aspect primary is evident in Gramsci's concern with children and language learning. He specifically advocated teaching children in their dialect. He wrote from prison to his sister urging her to let his nephew speak Sardinian. He showed great concern with how this language imposition could have harmful results developmentally and culturally if it resulted in disconnections between children and the communities and cultures in which they lived. He shows astute awareness of intellectual and identity issues concerning the *imposition* of 'foreign' languages. He also made the connection often central to the critics of 'global English' between language and culture and perceptions of the world, as opposed to viewing language solely as a conduit for communication.

Despite all these similarities with the critics of global English and his own rejection of Manzoni's method for creating a national Italian language, Gramsci was not against the creation of a truly 'common national Italian.' Quite the contrary, in no uncertain terms he proclaims: it is rational to collaborate practically and willingly to welcome everything that may serve to create a common national language, the non-existence of which creates friction particularly in the popular masses among whom local particularisms and phenomena of a narrow and provincial mentality are more tenacious than is believed.

Gramsci argues that the emergence of fascism was in part due to their ability to pit various subaltern groups against one another, especially the northern petit bourgeoisie against the working class, but also both of them against the southern peasantry. He thus agrees with the central point of supporters of 'global English' made by Van Parijs, that communication among disadvantaged social groups, marginalised and oppressed peoples is essential and its absence often facilitates dominant 'hegemonies' together with injustice. In such analyses, Gramsci is clearly more attuned to the political nature of the debate and the nuances of power dynamics than is Kachru, who commonly falls into more blanket assessments focusing on an overly positive outcomes of Asian Englishes. For example, he concurs with Thomas Friedman that India has successfully capitalised upon its ability to assimilate, synthesise and hybridise what is required of it by globalisation. And while at moments, he is acutely aware of the negative impacts of colonialism and on-going attempts like that of the British

Council to maintain the power of its cultural prestige, he also tends to put 'colonialism' in the past and argue that Indian English has been liberated from historical structures of imperialism.

However much Gramsci favours a common language for all of Italy in ways that resonate with Van Parijs' concerns and Archibugi's cosmopolitanism, he does not follow Van Parijs in separating language into two aspects, the communicative and the symbolic or cultural. Nor does his desire for a common language lead Gramsci ever to think of language providing a space for communication outside of questions of culture or power differentials and, in a word, politics. In a crucial section of the *Prison Notebooks,* Gramsci argues against the elitist conception of philosophy as "a strange and difficult thing" and turning Benedetto Croce's slogan, "all men are philosophers" on its head, Gramsci writes that spontaneous philosophy is contained in three things, 'common sense', 'the entire system of beliefs, superstitions, opinions, ways of seeing things, ... and, the first on the list, "*language itself,* which is a totality of determined notions and concepts not just words grammatically devoid of content". Later in the Notebooks, he writes, A Language also means culture and philosophy (if only at the level of common sense). Gramsci's diagnosis of the need for a truly 'common language' in Italy is due in large part to the connection between language as a vehicle for communication and as a crucial aspect of culture and identity.

Gramsci develops two concepts, they involved power relationships in any language learning and usage situation. They are 'spontaneous grammar' and 'normative grammar'. As is typical of Gramsci, he uses existing terms and modifies their meaning to make them more critical and often more analytic than how they had been used previously. He starts out by accepting the common notion that everyone speaks 'according to grammar' without necessarily knowing it. This 'immanent' or 'spontaneous' grammar is contrasted to 'normative grammar' with its long history dating back to Port-Royal. But Gramsci quickly breaks down this simplistic contrast between spontaneity and normativity. Thus, he argues that 'normative grammar' is: made up of reciprocal monitoring, reciprocal teaching and reciprocal 'censorship' expressed in such questions as 'What did you say?', 'What do you mean?', 'Make yourself clearer', etc. and in mimicry and teasing. This whole complex of actions and reactions come together to create a grammatical conformism, to establish 'norms' or judgments of correctness and incorrectness..

So here we have a clear picture of the power relationships involved in language learning which Gramsci further describes with examples of peasants moving to cities. To the extent that this is internalised, it becomes spontaneous, "One could sketch a picture of the 'normative grammar' that operates spontaneously in every given society, in that this society tends to become unified both territorially and culturally, in other words it has a governing class whose function is recognised and followed". Thus, no language is structured around a truly 'spontaneous' grammar that arises from nowhere or is divorced from the power relationships amongst its users. To the extent that language is structured making communication possible – and Gramsci describes this limit by connecting the etymology of 'idiot' with 'idiom' – it also involves the power relationship of some users controlling and defining the 'norms' by which others speak or write. The crucial thing is that for Gramsci, normative grammar is not simplistically aligned with force or coercion or domination and spontaneous grammar aligned with freedom and democracy. He actually argues that spontaneous grammar, those rules that we speak without thinking about them, are the historical result of fragmentation and sedimentation of various normative grammars.

Moreover, Gramsci argues that normative grammars always face pressures from the spontaneous grammars that someone speaks. This was another aspect of his critique of Manzoni. He argued that you could try to impose 'standard' Italian across Italy, but as you moved farther away from Tuscany and the dialects were more distinct from this new standard, speakers would continually change that standard. This is a very useful contribution to current debates on 'global English' however different from the context of Italian language 'standardisation' precisely because it does not deny, as so many proponents of 'global English' do, the fact that the communicative function of language is tied to the cultural choices and power dynamics amongst the users of that language. But it also does not valorise 'spontaneous' grammar or vernacular languages as somehow authentic or natural or even inherently more in tune with a particular group of people. For Gramsci, there is nothing akin to what Wilhelm von Humboldt called the *energia* of language that is unstructured prior to being expressed through the *ergon* of communal structure.

10.2. Communicational Benefits of 'Global English'

Gramsci then gives us more insight into what seems like a common sense proposition, that the spread of global English facilitates global communication. On one level, of course this is true. On another level, we have to ask two questions. Who specifically is engaging in this communication that stretches more frequently across wider portions of the globe? And what are the other larger contexts of this communication? How does miscommunication affect our lives and politics? Again, this assumption lies at the heart of De Swaan and Van Parijs' entire projects, as well as political theorists like Archibugi. And again, turning the Gramsci's writings provides some insight.

Prior to Gramsci's imprisonment, in 1918, he wrote a scathing article about Esperanto. He then developed 'Esperanto' and 'Esperantism' as metaphors in the *Prison Notebooks* to describe various positivistic and overly abstract philosophical positions especially in relation to science. In his initial critique, he criticised a proposal that the Milan section of the Communist Party adopt Esperanto. Gramsci rejects this proposal precisely because he sees the communicative function of language inextricable from the cultural questions. But he goes further problematising the very desire or need for a common or single lingua franca.

Thus, Gramsci interrogates the most prominent economic and class reasons that underlie the need for a 'world' language. Here he is critical of such a 'cosmopolitan' perspective because it presupposes class and cultural inequalities. This, of course, mirrors the dynamic that he develops more extensively in his *Prison Notebooks* with his concepts of a 'passive revolution' B a 'revolution' without a revolution B whereby superficial alterations are made to avoid the economic, social and political crises that are coming to the fore. But such 'passive revolutions' do not address the profound reasons for such crises.

Ultimately, Gramsci makes the argument that De Swaan, Archibugi and others side-step and ignore. Van Parijs, does touch on it. As Gramsci summarises: Every time that the question of language surfaces, in one way or another, it means that a series of other problems are coming to the fore: the formation and enlargement of the governing class, the need to establish more intimate and secure relationships between the governing groups and the national-popular mass, in other words to recognise the cultural hegemony.

10.3. Progressive Goals of Global English

Global English makes technical documents that are not slated for translation more readable for non-native speakers who are reasonably proficient in English. After all, many documents are never translated, and in today's world it is unusual for the audience of any technical document to consist solely of native speakers of English. Whether your audience consists primarily of scientists, engineers, software developers, machine operators, or unskilled workers, it probably includes a sizable number of non-native speakers.

Global English also makes documents clearer and more readable for native speakers, too. Because native speakers of English still constitute the majority of the audience for many technical documents, that benefit should not be overlooked. Depending on the type and subject matter of your documentation, Global English can provide the following benefits:

- Injuries, losses, and costly legal liabilities that can be caused by unclear documentation and by incorrect translations are avoided.
- Clearer, more-consistent documentation reduces calls to technical support.
- Consistent terminology facilitates the task of indexing and makes indexes more reliable.
- In online documentation or Help, users are better able to find the information they need because you have eliminated unnecessary synonyms and variant spellings.
- Translation quality is less of a concern because you have eliminated ambiguities and unnecessary complexities that can lead to mistranslations.

10.3.1. Global English for Professional Writers and Editors

Many professional writers and editors have recognised two benefits of Global English that are less relevant to authors whose main responsibilities are in other areas.

First, the ability to make documents more suitable for a global audience is a specialised and marketable skill. In a posting to a Society for Technical Communication mailing list, technical writer Richard Graefe made the following observation:

> With the increase in localisation of documentation and of user interfaces, being able to sell yourself as a person with "pre-localisation" editorial skills is a plus. To be able to do that type of editing well, you need . . . to be able to recognise English structures and expressions that will not translate well, that may be ambiguous to a translator, or that may require a translator to do rewriting in addition to translating.

The skills that Graefe described are exactly what this book helps you develop. In addition to giving job seekers a competitive edge, those skills could conceivably make professional writers and editors less vulnerable to layoffs and outsourcing. Second, editors often find that the Global English guidelines articulate issues that they could not have explained themselves. The same is true for writers who are working with technical information that was provided by subject-matter experts.

10.3.2. Cardinal Rule of Global English

Native speakers of English probably constitute a significant portion of the audience for much of your technical documentation. Therefore, be sure to follow the cardinal rule of Global English even while you are taking into account the needs of nonnative speakers and translators:

10.3.3. Language Technologies

Often, people who are interested in Global English are also interested in technologies that make global communication more efficient. Three language technologies that are machine-translation software, translation memory, and controlled-authoring software.

10.3.4. Machine-Translation Software

Machine-translation (MT) software is software that translates sentences from one language (such as English) into one or more other languages (such as French or Japanese). A guideline that improves the translated output for one MT system in one language might have a negligible effect (or, rarely, even a detrimental effect) for a different MT system or language. Before implementing machine-translation software, ask the software vendor to help you identify and prioritise the Global English guidelines that would make your documentation most suitable for that particular software. Also consult sources such as Bernth and Gdaniec, Roturier, and O'Brien and Roturier to gain a better understanding of how to evaluate the effect of specific guidelines on MT output.

10.3.5. Translation Memory

Virtually all technical translators use computer-assisted translation tools. One of the main components of these tools is translation memory (TM)—a database that stores the source language version and the target-language version of every sentence that is translated. When a new or updated document is processed by the software, any translation segments that are identical or similar to previously translated segments are presented to the translator. The translator then decides whether to reuse, modify, or disregard the previous translations.

Unnecessary inconsistencies make the use of translation memory less efficient. For example, suppose that a French translator translates the following sentence in the first edition of a software manual:

> Use the Group column to see if your tables are joined in more than one group.

Later, a translator who is using the TM database from that first edition encounters the same sentence in a new version of the document or in a related document. Instead of retranslating the sentence, the translator can insert the previous translation with the click of a mouse or with a keyboard shortcut.

Now suppose that the writer or editor who worked on the second edition of the manual had decided to modify that sentence as follows:

> Use the Group column to determine whether your tables are joined in more than one group.

In this scenario, the translation-memory software finds the translation of the original sentence in its database and presents that sentence and its translation to the translator as a fuzzy match. However, now the translator has to decide whether the previous translation is suitable or whether it needs to be modified. Obviously, that task is more cognitively demanding and more time-consuming than inserting the translation of an exact match. When the English sentence is ambiguous or difficult to understand, the task is especially time-consuming, and the decision process is subject to error. When you multiply the unnecessary variations in a document by the number of languages that the document will be translated into, the cost of those variations becomes very significant.

10.3.6. Controlled-Authoring Software

A controlled-authoring application parses texts and brings style errors, grammar errors, and terminology errors to the user's attention. One essential feature that distinguishes controlled-authoring software from other types of editing tools is that you can customise it. In collaboration with the software vendor, you can specify which grammar rules, style guidelines, and terminology restrictions you want the software to help authors follow.

You can also customise the rules to eliminate false alarms that are caused by idiosyncrasies in your documentation. Thus, the software is more accurate and reliable than off-the-shelf language checkers. Many organisations use controlled-authoring software to ensure a high degree of language quality and consistency in their publications; to increase the productivity of content authors, editors, and translators; to help non-native authors produce better-quality English source texts; or for other business reasons.

References

Anderson, B., *Imagined Communities,* London: Verso, 1991.

Archibugi, D., "The Language of Democracy: Vernacular or Esperanto? A Comparison Between the Multiculturalist and Cosmopolitan Perspectives," *Political Studies,* 2005.

Bishop, R. & J. Phillips, "Language" *Theory, Culture & Society,* 2006.

Boran, I., "Global Linguistic Diversity, Public Goods, and the Principle of Fairness," in W. Kymlicka & A. Patten, eds., *Language Rights and Political Theory,* Oxford: Oxford University Press, 2003.

Crowley, T., *Language in History: Theories and Texts,* London: Routledge, 1996.

Crystal, D., *English as a Global Language,* Cambridge: Cambridge University Press, 1997.

De Swaan, A., *Words of the World,* Cambridge: Polity, 2001.

Graddol, D., *English Next,* London: British Council, 2006.

Gramsci, A., *Selections from Cultural Writings,* D. Forgacs and G. Nowell-Smith, eds., W. Boelhower, trans., Cambridge: Harvard University Press, 1985.

Grin, F., "English as Economic Value: Facts and Fallacies", *World Englishes,* 2001.

Grin, F., "Diversity as Paradigm, Analytical Device, and Policy Goal," in W. Kymlicka & A. Patten, eds., *Language Rights and Political Theory,* Oxford: Oxford University Press, 2003.

Holborow, M., *The Politics of English,* London: Sage, 1999.

Ives, P., "Managing or Celebrating Linguistic Diversity?", *Working Paper,* 2004.

Ives, P., "Language, Representation, and Suprastate Democracy: Questions Facing the European Union" in D. Laycock, ed., *Representation and Democratic Theory,* Vancouver: UBC Press, 2004.

Ives, P., "Grammar" *Historical Materialism,* 2005.

Kymlicka, W. & A. Patten, *Language Rights and Political Theory,* Oxford: Oxford University Press, 2003.

Losonsky, M., *Linguistic Turns in Modern Philosophy,* Cambridge: Cambridge University Press, 2006.

May, S., "Misconceiving Minority Language Rights" in W. Kymlicka & A. Patten, eds., *Language Rights and Political Theory,* Oxford: Oxford University Press, 2003.

Patten, A., "Political Theory and Language Policy", *Political Theory,* 2001.

Pennycook, A., *The Cultural Politics of English as an International Language,* London: Longman, 1994.

_______________ ., "The Right to Language: Towards a Situated Ethics of Language Possibilities", *Language Sciences,* 1998.

Phillipson, R., *Linguistic Imperialism,* Oxford: Oxford University Press, 1992.

Seidlhofer, B. & J. Jenkins, "English as a Lingua Franca and the Politics of Property," in C. Mair, ed., *The Politics of English as a World Language* (Amsterdam: Rodopi), 2003.

Sonntag, S., *The Local Politics of Global English,* Lanham: Lexington Books, 2003.

Van Parijs, P., "Europe's Linguistic Challenge," *European Journal of Sociology,* 2004.

von Humboldt, W., *On Language,* P. Heath, trans., Cambridge: Cambridge University Press, 1988.

11
Future of English

English is the only global language available at such a fateful moment in history, is also being transformed. Inevitably, at the same time, the business of teaching and learning English is also changing beyond recognition. The relationships between stakeholders in the global English business learners, parents, governments, employers, publishers, schools—are also evolving rapidly. .

The next stage of global development will be as dramatic as that of the industrial revolution and the rise of nation states. We are rapidly shifting to a completely new social, economic and political order and with it a new world order in languages. English is proving to be a key part of this process. On the one hand, the availability of English as a global language is accelerating globalisation. On the other, the globalisation is accelerating the use of English.

Both postmodernity and global English have become mainstream features of the 21st century world. But it is only now that both are seriously transforming the world. This is the less exciting 'implementation' stage. The key period for this transitional stage is the next 10–15 years. In fact, we are probably already 5 years into a 20-year period of change. As the decade moves on, the world will look more like the future and less like the past.

11.1. Increasing Global Population

The world population then started rising fast. Cities in Europe expanded, sustained first by the agrarian revolution, which allowed greater food production with fewer workers, by the industrial revolution, which created new employment opportunities in towns, and by improvements in healthcare which reduced mortality rates. This trend towards population increase, industrialisation and urbanisation is still not completed in much of the world.

By the 1990s, population increase in many developed economies had slowed, but in less developed parts of the world it was still rising fast. The reasons for this imbalance lie in a complex mix of material circumstances, life chances and financial needs. In rural areas, children are important to family economies and as a future support for parents. In urban, middle class families children become more of a financial and lifestyle liability. This is one reason why populations grow more slowly as a country becomes more urbanised, middle class, and wealthy.

11.1.1. Changing Age Structure

One consequence of the rapid population growth in the developing world is that the age structure of countries varies considerably. In 2005, the median age in Italy was over 40 years, and getting higher year by year. Italy's problem is faced, albeit to a lesser extent, by many other countries in western Europe. In Uganda, on the other hand, the median age was under 15 years. In many developing countries, the number of children needing primary education is rising faster than governments can build new schools and train teachers.

11.1.2. Demographic Waves

It is not unusual to see age peaks and troughs in the age profile of a population as a 'baby boom' gives rise to a 'baby boomlet' a generation later. Such waves make capacity management at different educational levels tricky. On the whole, it is easier to increase the participation rate and introduce major curriculum innovations when a demographic cohort is declining in size. In Poland, for example, a demographic wave worked its way through the educational system in the last decade or so, but declining numbers of young people are entering school.

11.1.3. Patterns of Migration

Countries like Italy, facing declining numbers of young people in comparison with the numbers of elderly, are likely to receive large numbers of migrant workers to support the economy. This will in turn change the ethnic and linguistic profile of the country. On the other hand, countries which have rising numbers of people of working age, such as Poland, may experience high levels of emigration. Such migrant workers may acquire language skills which they bring back to the country at a future date.

11.1.4. People Movement

More people than ever are on the move. Between 1960 and 2000 the total number of international migrants had doubled to 175 million, representing nearly 3% of the world's population. Many migrants seek a better life in one of the more developed countries which encourage the immigration of skilled workers to counterbalance their ageing workforce. This is changing the social and linguistic mix of the destination countries. For example, London is now widely regarded as the most multilingual city in the world.

Freedom of labour movement within the EU has led to the emergence of new linguistic communities in many smaller English towns. After the accession of new countries to the European Union in 2005, Britain elected not to impose restrictions on migrant workers. The result has been an influx of workers from eastern Europe, especially Poland. In October 2005 the New York Times reported:

> Despite fears across Europe that low-cost workers would steal jobs, multicultural Britain has absorbed these workers with hardly a ripple . . . Poles, Lithuanians, Latvians and other Easterners are arriving at an average rate of 16,000 a month . . . Since May 2004, more than 230,000 East Europeans have registered to work in Britain.

In some parts of the UK, this influx has greatly increased demand for ESL classes, even in remote areas.

As the economies of developing countries grow, many former economic migrants return—often with the skills and capital they have acquired overseas. The governments of both China and India encourage 'returnees' who have become a new social category in these countries, part envied, part resented. Returnees usually face challenging issues relating to identity. Some family members of returnees may feel they belong 'elsewhere'—children, for example, who have been brought up in the USA with English as their first language.

International tourism is growing, but the proportion of encounters involving a native English speaker is declining. There were around 763 million international travellers in 2004, but nearly three-quarters of visits involved visitors from a non-English-speaking country travelling to a non-English-speaking destination. This demonstrates the scale of need for face-to-face international communication and a growing role for global English.

11.2. Economic Transformation

Economic relationships between the developed countries and those of the 'third world' are changing. Indian and Chinese economies, especially, have been growing fast. According to the OECD, China could overtake the USA and Germany to become the largest exporter in the world in the next 5 years. In December 2005, China revised its estimations of economic growth, showing that it had already overtaken Italy in GDP and was likely to become the world's fourth largest, overtaking the UK, by the end of 2006. China's services sector was particularly underestimated and probably already accounts for over 40% of its GDP.

Services are of linguistic interest since they often require much higher levels of communication than manufacturing. Exported services—which include receiving international students and tourists—often require international communication. The trade imbalance in services across all developing countries seems to be falling, which reflects the increasingly two-way direction of economic and communicative flows.

The world economy is experiencing the impact of two new economic superpowers emerging simultaneously. But it is not just China and India whose economies are growing fast.

11.2.1. Impact of Globalisation

Globalisation allows companies to locate each of their activities wherever in the world provides the best cost advantage. The ideal global business plan is thus one in which products can be manufactured in countries where labour is cheap and sold into markets where people are rich. During the 1990s, the manufacture of goods of all kinds, from t-shirts to mobile phones, shifted to countries with low labour costs. This created a deflationary effect on developed economies.

Many services are now outsourced, in the same way as the manufacture of computers or t-shirts. Such business process outsourcing (BPO) and information technology outsourcing (ITO) are not a new phenomenon. Many operations such as company payroll or specialist computer data processing, have been subcontracted by companies to specialised bureaux since the 1960s. What has changed is the huge range of services which are now affected, and the fact that cheap communications allow many of them to be carried out in distant locations. The trend is now clear: if there is any fraction of a service which can be separated from a physical location and done more cheaply somewhere else, it will be outsourced.

Call centres, in which service calls from members of the public are picked up in a distant country such as India, have attracted much public attention—and even led some companies to advertise the fact they are relocating call centres 'back home'. However, call centres account for a small percentage of the BPO market. According to the OECD, close to 20% of total employment in the 15 pre-expansion EU countries, America, Canada and Australia, could 'potentially be affected' by the international sourcing of services activities.

11.2.2. Knowledge Economy

Each country maintains its competitive advantage as a destination for outsourcing only for a relatively short time. As investment pours into the country, and demand for labour rises, so inevitably do wage and property costs. Taiwan, Singapore, Malaysia and Hong Kong all used to be favourite places for the manufacture of computer parts but much of the business has now shifted to mainland China.

The services sector is proving to be even more volatile. As wage costs inevitably rise in the main hubs of India, call centres are relocated to smaller cities—with lower costs, poorer communication infrastructure and poorer English skills. This allows other countries to compete to become the next wave of BPO centres: from Bulgaria to Nicaragua, from Vietnam to Belarus. Some of the new destinations are actually being developed by large Indian BPO enterprises: India, like China, is itself now globalising. Some global enterprises run their own 'captive' operations. HSBC, for example, can select whichever of its many outsourcing centres at a given time has the best mix of skills and costs for a particular contract. Because multinationals establish outsourcing centres in several countries as part of their global risk management, they can shift work from one country to another very quickly, allowing them to maintain competitive advantage themselves.

11.2.3. Redistribution of Poverty

One of the legacies of the British Empire is that, in many countries, access to English remains part of an elitest social process. In the old, modernist model, English proficiency acted as a marker of membership of a select, educated, middle class group. In a globalised world, English is much more widely distributed, as is access to education generally. The increasingly important role that English is now playing in economic processes, in providing access to the kind of global knowledges available in English and the jobs which involve contact with customers and colleagues for whom English is the only shared language, has brought with it the danger that English has become one of the main mechanisms for structuring inequality in developing economies. Lack of English in some countries now threatens to exclude a minority rather than the majority of a population.

11.3. Future Technology

By the end of the 20th century, the cost of a call was determined less by distance and duration and more by the extent to which the telecoms business in a destination country had been liberalised. Countries such as Vietnam were amongst the most costly to reach from the UK, whereas the English-speaking world had been brought into close proximity, in terms of 'teledistance'.

In 2004, international calls from fixed lines reached 140 billion minutes. In 2002, mobile phone connections overtook fixed lines and passed the 2 billion figure in September 2005. With the development of voice over internet protocol (VOIP), calls can be made over the internet across the world at no marginal cost. Such facilities are not only available to large corporations—making Indian call centres more attractive—but also to ordinary consumers through schemes such as Skype which, by the end of 2005, claimed to have 50 million users. VOIP is replacing landline technology, which is expected to be obsolete in the UK by 2010.

11.3.1. Text Messaging

Short text messages (SMS) have become a major form of communication in Europe and Asia, especially among young people. SMS has had several social and political impacts: in the UK new forms of bullying have emerged; in Germany, it is used to organise mass parties. In 2001, text massaging helped bring down the Philippines President, Joseph Estrada; in 2005, it helped mobilise participants in the 'Orange revolution' in the Ukraine, and massive anti-Syrian protests in Lebanon after the assassination of former Prime Minister Rafk Hariri.

11.3.2. Surveillance Society

Technology is undermining the traditional distribution of power by redistributing knowledge. The state builds databases on its citizens; businesses profile the buying habits of their customers through loyalty cards; surveillance cameras provide data on civil disturbances, crime, weather and traffic flow; eavesdropping technologies monitor citizens conversations, email and text messages or comments on websites. Citizens exploit the same technologies. Internet forums allow shoppers to compare prices and read consumer reviews; volunteers create databases of the location of speed cameras for use in car navigation systems; blogs, websites, and webcams allow individuals and small communities to project and manage their own identities.

11.3.3. Language on the Internet

In 1998, Geoff Nunberg and Schulze found that around 85% of web pages were in English. The dominance of English on the internet has probably been overestimated. What began as an anglophone phenomenon has rapidly become a multilingual affair. Software has been made capable of displaying many different kinds of script. Many corporate websites now employ multilingual strategies making choice of language a 'user preference'. Machine translation of web content is only a mouse-click away. And there are many reasons why the internet, which started as a long-distance, global communications medium, is now serving much more local interests. Furthermore, the internet is proving to be a very useful resource to those interested in learning lesser-used languages.

11.3.4. News Media

In a globalised world international news plays a crucial role in ensuring that citizens and businesses are kept aware of developments affecting their lives and decisionmaking. For too long, perhaps, international news has been dominated by English language providers such as Associated Press, Reuters, the BBC or CNN; channels which have sought to position themselves as the places to tune to during a major breaking story. However, recent trends will diversify both the viewpoints available in international news in English, and the languages in which global news is provided.

When Al Jazeera started broadcasting from its base in Qatar at the end of 1996, it triggered a transformation of the international news media. By providing an independent source of news about events in the Middle East, it managed to discomfort equally both western governments and those in neighbouring Arab states. Arabic suddenly became an important language in which to present world news. A rival news channel, Al Arabiya, began transmitting in 2003 from Dubai, with Saudi backing. In early 2004, Al Hurra, a new Arabic news channel funded by the US government began transmitting to 22 Arab countries from its Washington studios.

Latin America launched its own, Spanish language, rival to CNN when, on 31 October 2005, Telesur began full broadcasting from Caracas. English, however, remains the preferred language for global reach. Al Jazeera plans to go global in English, establishing regional headquarters in London, Washington and Kuala Lumpur. By the end of 2005, its English website had become a major source of news for American internet users and its new English language TV channel is expected to start broadcasting in spring 2006. Russia's new government-funded, English-language 24-hour TV channel 'Russia Today' began broadcasting in December 2005, to North America, Europe and Asia. Even France's new global channel, due by the end of 2006, will broadcast in both French and English, following the successful bilingual model of the German international channel, Deutsche Welle. And a new pan-African news channel—using French and English—is planned.

11.3.4.1. Blogs

By the end of 2005, there were an estimated 20 million active blogs worldwide. Some bloggers now act as independent journalists, breaking stories which are taken up by the mainstream media. Others have acquired large readership for their blogs and become influential opinion leaders. Blogs also provide a public record of grassroots experience—for example, the progress of hurricanes across the USA. Trend analysis shows what people are discussing from day to day. Independent citizen–journalists do not just break stories, but also act as an army of fact-checkers who will call to account any news source who gets their facts wrong. Technology also allows mainstream media, such as the BBC, to tap in to citizen news gatherers. Not only can people around the world file their own accounts of breaking news stories via the internet, but also upload photos which they have taken with their camera phones.

11.4. Society

An increasing proportion of the world's population will be city dwellers. A developing economy seems to require urbanisation, and as an economy develops workers flood in to the cities. The rate of urbanisation in China, despite the size of its rural population, is one of the highest in the world, and a further 300 million people are expected to move to the cities in the coming decade. Urbanisation is not the same as population density—in most countries urbanisation leads to depopulation of the countryside and changing patterns of land use. English, however, is an increasingly urban language, associated with growing middle classes, metropolitan workplaces and city lifestyles. The middle class is not just a consequence of a growing economy, but also a contributory factor. Both Indian and Chinese governments see the enlargement of the middle classes as a means of increasing domestic consumption and so attracting inward investment from multinational companies, whilst providing a stabilising effect on society.

In the mid-1980s less than 10% of the Indian population was regarded as middle class, and only half of those were English speakers. The Indian middle class has since grown dramatically—to around 20% or 220 million people. Lifestyle changes, however, have evolved even faster, especially in the main metropolitan cities. Urbanisation in India has been slower than in many other parts of Asia and hence the linguistic impact has been less. Much of the focus of the new economy has been in the south—in cities such as Bangalore which has long embraced English as a defence against the perceived linguistic hegemony of northern Hindi. However, it appears that recent improvements to India's road network is making it easier for rural population to reach neighbouring large towns and this may be consolidating the position of Hindi.

The rise of a middle class in China is a fairly recent phenomenon—some say it appeared only in the late 1990s, others that it will require a level of 50% urbanisation and at least 50% of the economy to be based on services, before a true middle class can evolve. Using a definition based on income alone, around 19% of China's population was considered to be middle class in 2003, and this is expected to grow to 40% by 2020.

By no means all city-dwellers are middle class—only about half, in present-day China. Mass migration to the cities often gives rise to slums on their outskirts, constraining further growth. But such communities are typically multilingual, drawn from different parts of the country or containing large immigrant populations. And while inequalities of wealth may emerge between countryside and city, many city workers remain ambassadors for rural families, acting as a conduit for cultural and economic flows between rural and urban areas. The scale of such urban-rural ties in China was demonstrated during the annual Spring Festival at the end of January, 2006. One estimate suggested that 'up to two billion journeys' were made within the country, including those of over 120 million migrant workers and students making the often arduous journeys back to their families elsewhere in the country.

11.4.1. Social Cohesion

As many developed countries become the destination for migrants, the ethnic mix is changing and with it fears of the erosion of national identity, as represented in a shared national language and values. Anxiety is growing about what appears to be the increasing separateness of some ethnic communities.

In cities in North America and western Europe, it may not be necessary to be fluent in the national language in order to find work or obtain access to key services, including shopping, healthcare and voting. Ethnic communities may be sufficiently large to be self-sustaining and public services increasingly cater for linguistic minorities.

There is another side to such separate, parallel lives. In premodernity, there was little movement of individuals. Aside from periods of mass migration, only particular classes travelled: some kinds of trader, explorer, soldiers, entertainers, scholar-monks. In modernity, travel became easier as technology improved. European empires involved much coming and going, and emigration to the new colonies. During wartime, large numbers of people came into contact with new cultures and languages. But by and large, once individuals and families moved, they also moved on, leaving behind old relationships and starting a new life and identity.

We now live in a world in which migrants do not have to break connections with friends and family to begin the generations-long process of assimilating to a new identity. Not only is it possible to retain close contact with the 'home' community, on a daily basis via email and telephone, it is also possible for people to read the same newspapers as those being read in the community they have left, watch the same television programmes on satellite television, or borrow the same films on DVD.

Furthermore, we can see with the perspective of the 21st century that patterns of emigration are now reversable. Chinese or Indian immigrants who intended to make new lives in America—even adopting citizenship may none the less return to their native countries, bringing with them young families who did not grow up there.

References

Block, D. and Cameron, D., (eds), *Globalization and Language Teaching,* London: Routledge, 2002.

Brutt-Giffl er, J., *World English: a study in its development,* Clevedon: Multilingual Matters, 2002.

Crystal, D., *English as a Global Language,* Cambridge: Cambridge University Press, 1997.

de Swaan, A., *Words of the World,* Cambridge: Polity, 2001.

Gnutzmann, C. and Intemann, F., (eds) *The Globalisation of English and the English Language Classroom,* Tübingen: Gunter Narr Verlag, 2005.

Graddol, D., *The Future of English?,* London: British Council, 1997.

Jenkins, J., *The Phonology of English as an International Language,* Oxford: Oxford University Press, 2000.

McKay, S. L., *Teaching English as an International Language: rethinking goals and approaches,* Oxford: Oxford University Press, 2002.

Phillipson, R., *Linguistic Imperialism,* Oxford: Oxford University Press, 1992.

Maurais, J. (ed.), *Languages in a Globalising World,* Cambridge: Cambridge University Press, 2006.

Bibliography

Adamson, B., *China's English: A history of English in Chinese education*, Hong Kong SAR, China: University of Hong Kong Press, 2004.

Ammon, Ulrich, "The status of German and other Languages in the European Community", In: Coulmas, Florian (ed.) *A Language Policy for the European Community: Prospects and Quandaries*, Berlin.: De Gruyter, 1991.

_______________ ., "Towards more fairness in international English: Linguistic rights of non-native speakers", In R. Phillipson (Ed.), *Rights to language. Equity, power, and education*, Mahwah, N.J.: Lawrence Erlbaum, 2000.

Bailey, Richard W., *Images of English: a cultural History of the Language*, Cambridge: CUP, 1991.

Bamgbose, A., *"Torn between the norms: innovations in world Englishes"*, World Englishes, 1998.

Baron, N., "Letters by phone or speech by other means: The linguistics of email", *Language and Communication*, 1998.

Baron, N.S., *Alphabet to email: How written English evolved and where it's heading*, New York: Routledge, 2000.

Barr, T., *The changing face of Australia's media and communications*, Sidney, Australia: Allen and Unwin, 2000.

Baudrillard, J., *The violence of the global*, (F. Debrix, Trans.), Paris: Galilee, 2002.

Baugh, Albert C, Thomas Cable, *A history of the English language*, 5th ed., Routledge, 2002.

Berns, M., & Friedrich, P. (Eds.), "Special issue on English in South America: A different kind of difference", [Special issue], *World Englishes*, 2003.

Bhatia, V.K., *Analysing Genre: Language Use in Professional Settings*, London: Longman, 1993.

Biber, D., Johansson, S., Leech, G., Conrad, S. & Finegan, E., *Longman Grammar of Spoken and Written English*, Harlow, Essex: Pearson, 1999.

Block, D. and Cameron, D., (eds), *Globalization and Language Teaching*, London: Routledge, 2002.

Block, D., *The social turn in second language acquisition*, Edinburgh, Scotland: University of Edinburgh Press, 2003.

Bolton, K., "World Englishes", In A. Davies & C. Elder (Eds.), *The handbook of applied linguistics*, Oxford, England: Blackwell, 2004.

Bragg, Melvyn, *The Adventure of English: The Biography of a Language*, Arcade Publishing, 2004.

Brann, Conrad M.B., "Lingua minor, franca & nationalis", In: Ammon, Ulrich (ed.), *Status and Function of Languages and Language Varieties*, Berlin: de Gruyter, 1989.

Braudel, F., *Civilization and Capitalism 15th-18th century*, London, UK: William Collins and Sons, 1983.

Brumfit, C.J. (ed.), *English for International Communication*, Oxford: Pergamon, 1982.

Brumfit, C.J., *Individual Freedom in Language Teaching: Helping Learners to Develop a Dialect of their Own*, Oxford: Oxford University Press, 2001.

Bruthiaux, Paul, "Squaring the Circles: Issues in Modeling English Worldwide", *International Journal of Applied Linguistics*, 2003.

Brutt-Giffl er, J., *World English: a study in its development*, Clevedon: Multilingual Matters, 2002.

Brutt-Griffler, J., *World English*, Clevedon: Multilingual Matters, 2002.

Buttjes, D. & Byram, M. (eds.), *Mediating Languages and Cultures: Towards an Intercultural Theory of Foreign Language Education*, Clevedon: Multilingual Matters, 1990.

Canagarajah, S., *Resisting linguistic imperialism in English teaching*, Oxford, England: Oxford University Press, 1999.

Candlin, C. N., & Mercer, N., *English language teaching in its social contexts: A reader*, London: Routledge, 2001.

Cheshire Jenny (ed.), *English Around the World: Sociolinguistic Perspectives*, Cambridge University Press, 1991.

Crystal, David, *English as a Global Language*, Cambridge: Cambridge University Press, 1997.

______________ ., *Language and the Internet*, Cambridge: Cambridge University Press, 2001.

______________ , *The Cambridge encyclopedia of the English language*, 2nd ed., Cambridge University Press, 2003.

______________ , *English as a Global Language*, Cambridge University Press, Cambridge, UK, 2006.